AF646472

THE SĀHITYAKAṆṬAKODDHĀRA

THE
SĀHITYAKAṆṬAKODDHĀRA

Edited with Introduction and Notes by

T. VENKATACHARYA

Professor of Sanskrit, University of Toronto, Canada

MOTILAL BANARSIDASS

Delhi :: Varanasi :: Patna

First Edition : Delhi, 1980

© MOTILAL BANARSIDASS PUBLISHERS PRIVATE LIMITED
All Rights Reserved

ISBN: 978-81-2082-779-0

Also available at:

MOTILAL BANARSIDASS

41 U.A. Bungalow Road, Jawahar Nagar, Delhi 110 007
8 Mahalaxmi Chamber, Warden Road, Mumbai 400 026
120 Royapettah High Road, Mylapore, Chennai 600 004
Sanas Plaza, Subhash Nagar, Pune 411 002
16 St. Mark's Road, Bangalore 560 001
8 Camac Street, Calcutta 700 017
Ashok Rajpath, Patna 800 004
Chowk, Varanasi 221 0011

PRINTED IN INDIA

BY JAINENDRA PRAKASH JAIN AT SHRI JAINENDRA PRESS,
A-45 NARAINA, PHASE I, NEW DELHI 110 028
AND PUBLISHED BY NARENDRA PRAKASH JAIN FOR
MOTILAL BANARSIDASS PUBLISHERS PRIVATE LIMITED,
BUNGALOW ROAD, DELHI 110 007

The editor is happy to record his grateful acknowledgements to the *Canada Council* for their Research Grants, which have enabled him to visit different Libraries in India, and work on the *Sāhityakaṇṭakoddhāra*.

T. Venkatacharya

CONTENTS

ABBREVIATIONS

A.R.	*Anargharāghava*; N.S.P. edn. 1937
H.C.S.L.	*History of Classical Sanskrit Literature*, by M. Krishnamachariar, Delhi, 1970
H.S.P.	*History of Sanskrit Poetics*; P.V. Kane; 1961
K.A.S.V.	*Kāvyālaṃkārasūtra* & *Vṛtti*; Vāṇīvilāsa edn.
K.P.	*Kāvyaprakāśa*; Jhalakīkar; Poona, 1965
P.M.	*Prauḍhamanoramā* on the *Siddhānta-kaumudī*; Chowkhamba, 1939
Ś.K.	*Śabdakaustubha* of Bhaṭṭoji; Chow-khamba edn.
S.K.	*Vaiyākaraṇasiddhāntakaumudī* of Bhaṭṭoji; Delhi
S.P.	*Sanskrit Poetics*; by S. K. De; Calcutta, 1960
T.B.	*Tattvabodhinī* on the *Siddhāntakaumudī*; Delhi

Other standard works are also consulted. See also the list of works and authors mentioned in the *S.K.U.*, which is supplied in the Introduction.

INTRODUCTION

I. The author of the *Sāhityakaṇṭakoddhāra*

In his *History of Classical Sanskrit Literature* M. Krishnamachariar mentions on page 789 one Madhusūdana as the author of the *Sāhityakaṇṭakoddhāra* (hereafter abbreviated *S.K.U.*). He does not supply any source or basis for this information about the name of the author. But, I do not find any name of the author at all in the manuscripts (7 in all) I have collated for the present edition.

In the verse 9 at the beginning (*nityaṃ vaidyaka-śāstra* etc.) the author mentions Nārāyaṇa as his father. This Nārāyaṇa is also described, in the same verse, to have been a dedicated master, who was always bent on explaining clearly the hidden meanings of the texts on the science of medicine (i.e. *Āyurveda-śāstra*). He is further referred to as *śrīvatsānvaya-bhūṣaṇa*, i.e. an ornament or a gem in the family belonging to the *Śrīvatsagotra*. The mother of the author is described to have been a symbol or a protector of the *pativratādharma*, and according to some her name is Dharmāvatī, though the present editor is not convinced about[1] it. Nothing is conveyed about her parents or the family. In verse 8, the author speaks highly about two of his ancestors, mentions them as *Koneri-Viṭṭhalabudhau* and says that they were experts in expounding the science of medicine, who surpassed in the proficiency even the twin divine physicians (Aśvinīdevas). They, it is

1. See Note 17-b to the text, and the verse 9 in this connection.

stated further, were great scholars in the *Sāhitya-śāstra* (i.e. Poetics) and were also like two peaks of the golden mountain of the *Śrīvatsagotra*.

Regarding the expression *Koneri-Viṭṭhalabudhau*, the following may be noted. From my namesake and a friend Śrī Venkatacharya who is a Senior Sanskrit Pandit in the Government Oriental Manuscripts Library, Madras, I learn that (according to *Guruparamparā-prabhāva*,[2] p. 301, line 15—a work in Tamil printed in Telugu script —from which he read out to me) the word *Koneru*, a Telugu word belonging to the Dravidian family, originally stood for the *Svāmipuṣkariṇī* — the pond attached to the Temple on the Tirumala Hills (near Tirupati in Āndhra Pradesh) of which the presiding Deity is the Lord Veṅkateśvara. Lord Veṅkateśvara is regarded as a form of Viṣṇu, is worshipped by many devoted Hindus even now, and is the family Deity of the present Editor also. The word Koneru came subsequently to be used as a name for the place (i.e. Tirumala Hills). Being connected with the sacred place, this expression came to be given as a name to a person by the devotees of Veṅkaṭeśvara. Perhaps the ancestors of our author were devotees of Viṣṇu, as is indicated by the practice. Generally these names are found among the Vaiṣṇavas in South India (e.g. among the followers of *Viśiṣṭādvaita* and *Dvaita* schools, and not found among Advaitins). Koneru or Koneri (a derivative meaning "belonging to Koneru") *plus* Ayya (which came from *Ārya*) results in Konerayya. In the Italian language Venti *plus* uno becomes *ventuno* (twenty-one). This we may call a *pararūpasandhi*, i.e. of the two

2. *Guruparamparāprabhāva* by Pinnaḷagiya Jeeyar; published in the year *Kali* 5011 (A.D. 1910); Kānchīpuram, Gitacharya Press.

vowels in euphony the second remains, whereas the first is elided. Similarly the expression *Konerayya* is a case of the *Pararūpasandhi*, which *sandhi* is common in the Telugu language. Like Italian words, Telugu words also end in Vowels. Professor (in English) is Professore in Italian. *Manas* and *śiras* of Sanskrit, for example are *Manasu* and *śirasu* in Telugu. These two similar points, i.e. words ending in Vowels, and the existence of the *Pararūpasandhi* may have been, in addition to other reasons, responsible for the saying that the Telugu is the Italian of the East. Koneri-budha or Konerayya seems similar in significance to Tirumalācārya (the author of the *Ratnaśāṇa* on the *Pratāparudrīya*) or the short form Tirumalayya (from Tirumalārya), which names are common among the people in the Telugu area.

Viṭṭhalācārya, Viṭṭhalārya and Viṭṭhalayya are also known names in South India. Viṭṭhala is the name of a form of Viṣṇu or Kṛṣṇa worshipped at Pandharpur in Bombay, says Apte in his Dictionary (q.v.).

Thus Koneri-budha (or Konerayya) and Viṭṭhala-budha (or Viṭṭhalācārya) refer to the two scholars with these names, it seems to me, who were the ancestors and belonged to the *Śrīvatsagotra* of which family the author of the *S.K.U.* was also a descendant, as is made clear in the next verse. In this manner, the names of Koneri-budha, Viṭṭhala-budha and (*tātas tu*) Nārāyaṇa are all found in the Introductory verses. But, the name Madhusūdana as the name of the author of the *S.K.U.* is not at all available in the MSS I had access to. It is not clear how and from where M. Krishnamachariar got hold of Madhusūdana.

Probably the author chose to remain anonymous, and because of this consideration perhaps even in the colophons no name of the author is found. This is simply my surmise, and till we get some positive evidence it is difficult to have any definite information about the name of the author of the *S.K.U.*

Our author does not seem to have any sectarian bias against one or the other of the Hindu gods, as seen in the case of some writers of the recent centuries. He pays his obeisance to Sarasvatī in verse 1, to Viṣṇu in verse 2, to Śiva in verses 3, 4, and 5, to Pāṇḍuraṅga (i.e. Viṣṇu) in verse 6, and finally to Gaṇeśa in verse 7.

II. *The Date of the Author*

It is equally difficult to have any definite information about the date of our anonymous author. Verse 10 of the *S.K.U.* reads thus :

granthaśikṣāśataṃ vīkṣya granthikān upasevya ca,
sāhityakaṇṭakoddhāraṃ nāma granthaṃ karomy aham.

This reminds us of Deveśvara who says in his *Kavikalpalatā* thus :

kaviśikṣāśataṃ vīkṣya kavīndrān upajīvya ca,
nibaddheyaṃ mayā dhīrās tvaritaślokasiddhaye.

(A.S.B., 1913; I.5)

Not only this. Deveśvara says thus also :

yad anyair vartma na kṣuṇṇaṃ tatra saṃcarato mama,
pade pade praskhalatas santas santv avalambanam.

(*Ibid.* I.4)

Now let us see what the author of the *S.K.U.*, has. He says (Verse 11) :

na kṣuṇṇo'yaṃ parair mārgas tatra saṃcarato mama,
pade pade praskhalatas santas santv avalambanam.

In fact, see the very first verse of the *S.K.U.* which reads thus :

saṃsāramarusaṃcāratṛṣitānāṃ śarīriṇām,
sudhākādambinībhūtaṃ tan mahas samupāsmahe.

Compare this with what Deveśvara has in the following :

saṃsāramarusaṃcārasamudbhūtaprabhūtakhedānāṃ
tāpatrayātapataptānām asmākam akasmād ajani
sudhākādambinīkadambasambandhaḥ.

(K.K.L., 1923; p. 139)

It seems clear from these that our author had received effective inspiration from Deveśvara. *S.K.U.* also quotes the line

gaja iva paramahelāvilāsī

(*Ibid.* p. 92)

with the words *iti Kavikalpalatāyām* (See *S.K.U.* p. 60).

Deveśvara was assigned to the beginning of the 14th century. (See S. K. De's *History of Sanskrit Poetics*, p. 260). Our author quotes (see p. 46) a verse from one *Narasiṃhacampū*, which was perhaps the same as the one attributed to Sūryakavi, who wrote the commentary *Bālabodhikā* on the *Kavikalpalatā*. (See S. K. De; *Ibid.* p. 262). From this we need not take that our author came soon after Deveśvara or Sūryakavi. He seems to be much later for the following reasons.

In verse 12, he declares *nāmūlaṃ likhyate kiṃcit* (which is on the model of Mallinātha). In keeping with this declaration, we notice, all the comments that he makes are made on the authority of many standard works like the *Śabdakaustubha* of Bhaṭṭoji, and the name of *Śabdakaustubha* is also mentioned in one place (see p. 6). He follows the *Prauḍhamanoramā* and the *Tattvabodhinī* too, though he does not mention these names. These references are supplied in the Footnotes. See for instance Notes 206, 207, and 220. There are several places where the *Śabdakaustubha*, the *Prauḍhamanoramā*, the *Siddhānta-kaumudī* are utilized by our author. A reference is found to a *Kāvyaprakāśakhaṇḍanakāra*, which does not seem to be to Siddhicandragaṇi, but it may be to *Śrīvatsalāñchana-bhaṭṭācārya* (See Note 32). Śrīvatsa-lāñchana was earlier than Jagannātha who refers to him by name in his *Rasagaṅgādhara* (p. 39; N.S.P.). Though there is no mention of the *Tattvabodhinī* or Jñānendrasarasvatī, our author seems to have been either a contemporary or even later than Jñānendra-sarasvatī. Our author quotes one foot of a verse thus :

prabhus tu vibudhāśrayaḥ kati na santi kukṣiṃbharāḥ,
(p. 54)

of which the full verse is found in the *Tattvabodhinī*, but no reference to this verse is found in the *Śabda-kaustubha* (See N. 211). The quoted part of the verse is attributed by our author to one Ḍhakkārāmakavi. It is not clear as to whether it could be a reference to Gururāmakavi of Diṇḍima family. The date of Gururāma's *Hariścandracarita* is said to be 1607 A.D. See Note 211. The *Tattvabodhinī* which gives the full verse does not mention the name of the author of the verse. The verse which is not found in the *Śabdakaustubha*, is perhaps not available in the *Prauḍhamanoramā* too. I have no access to the related volume of the *Prauḍhamanoramā* here. Perhaps our author is quoting the verse from the *Tattvabodhinī*, and the answer to the problem connected with the usage *kukṣiṃbhara* in the context is given in the *Tattvabodhinī*, which is referred to by our author by the expression *ity eke*. There are certain other places too where the *S.K.U.* seems to be following the *Tattvabodhinī*.

Jñānendrabhikṣu (or Jñānendrasarasvatī) is said to have been a Teacher, in the Vedānta, of the father of Jagannātha, who is assigned to the period between 1590 and 1665 A.D. There is no reference to Jagannātha, as far as I can search, in the *S.K.U.*, and this absence of reference need not mean anything. Jagannātha did not have any systematic discussion about the correctness or otherwise of linguistic uses in literary works, with which our author is mainly concerned here. The absence of any reference, therefore, to Jagannātha need not mean an earlier date for our author. There is no mention of Nāgeśa or his works in the *S.K.U.* But in one place there is similarity of views of our author and of Nāgeśa (See Note 143). Our author was probably a contemporary of Nāgeśa, and belonged to the time by which Nāgeśa's works had not yet travelled to the other parts of the country. Though our author refers to some *Paribhāṣās* (See pp. 51, 52 and 53) there is no reference to the *Paribhāṣenduśekhara*. See also Notes 57, 205. If it was known, I think that the author would have been tempted to make a reference to it by name. The author of the *S.K.U.*, therefore, probably belonged to the latter part of the 17th century or the beginning of the 18th century.

III. *The title and the subject of the S.K.U.*

The *S.K.U.* does not seem to be intended by the author to serve as a work on *Kaviśikṣā* (i.e. a manual of instructions to those aspiring to become poets). It is exegetical in nature, but belongs to the field of "*Grammar as an Applied Science*". It is similar to the section on *śabdaśuddhi* in the *Kāvyālaṃkārasūtra-vṛtti* of Vāmana. The sixth chapter in Bhāmaha's *Kāvyālaṃkāra*, the *Prāyogikādhikaraṇa* (last section) of Vāmana, *Durghaṭavṛtti*, and the anonymous *Mukha-bhūṣaṇa* are only a few works that have a systematic treatment pointing out the correctness or otherwise of the usages of the Poets. The *Mukhabhūṣaṇa*, which is not known to our author, has a good compilation mostly based on Vāmana's, and sometimes on other authoritative works on grammar, and it has also some new and interesting comments of the anonymous author himself. The 7th chapter of the *Kāvyapra-kāśa* and the *S. D.*, which is based on *K. P.*, have some grammatical discussions on one or two points such as the *sandhi*, and the use of *Parasmaipada* or the *Ātmanepada* etc. Compared to the bulk of works dealing with other literary aspects, the (above-noted) works on *śabdaśuddhi* are very few. This is what seems to be intended by our author when he says:

na kṣuṇṇo'yaṃ parair mārgaḥ (verse 11).

To the list, which was illustrative and not exhaustive, of the usages of the Poets noted by previous writers like Bhāmaha, and Vāmana, our author has added some more expressions with his own discussions. In keeping with his declaration *nāmūlaṃ likhyate* in verse 12, he has all his discussions corroborated by the authoritative works like the *Mahābhāṣya*, *Kāśikā*, *Nyāsa*, *Padamañjarī*, *Kaiyaṭapradīpa*, *Śabdakaustubha* etc. He seems to have very high opinion about Bhaṭṭoji to whom he refers with the terms as *Bhāṣyarahasyajña*, (pp. 8, 24) and *Bhāṣyamanthanakartṛ* (p. 29).

As is made clear by the title (*S.K.U.*), in the opinion of our author the incorrect or incorrect-looking usages of Poets are like thorns (i.e. *kaṇṭaka*) on the path of the *sāhitya*. He has tried to clear the path of these thorns. Though majority of the uses are collected from the *Kāvyas*, there are some expressions culled also from other sources such as the *Rāmāyaṇa*, *Mahābhārata*, the *Smṛti* texts, *Devīmāhātmya* (This is discussed by Bhaṭṭoji and others too) some *Madhukośa*, works on *Vaidyaśāstra*, *Jyotiśśāstra* and *Vāyavyapurāṇa* (See the Index) etc. It is because of this fact that he seems to have chosen the word *Sāhitya* etc. instead of *Kāvyakaṇṭakoddhāra*. The word *sāhitya* was understood in the sense of literature in general.

The Introductory verses show that the author was capable of composing some good poetic pieces. See particularly the verse 4 (*mūrdhni sthitām* etc.).

IV. *The role played by the present work*

The author has accurate knowledge of the contents and the context of the verses he has quoted. He has a dependable knowledge of standard works on grammar such as the *Mahābhāṣya*, the *Kāśikā*, *Nyāsa*, *Padamañjarī*, *Śabdakaustubha* etc. His interpretations and applications of grammatical rules are reliable. He refers to some interesting views about the *sandhi* and *saṃhitā*. See Notes 26, 29 and 30, for the details. He is quite familiar with the well-known *Mahākāvyas*. Though some of the expressions he notes were also explained in brief by earlier writers like Vāmana, and some commentators on the *Mahākāvyas*, he has his own comments which he conveys by using *vayaṃ paryālocayāmaḥ* etc. (See pp. 20 and 21, 60). He has to his credit also some entirely new expressions which were not noted by other writers. For instance, the following were not noted either by Vāmana or the author of the *Mukhabhūṣaṇa* (Adyar Publication 1973) :

1. *adhimat* p. 20; Note 84
2. *āpya* p. 34; N. 133
3. *āvis* (The position of) p. 23; Note 99
4. *ūditha* p. 42; N. 162-164
5. *kalāstanmayāḥ* p. 34; N. 134
6. *tyajasva* p. 43
7. *niścotante* p. 39; N. 153
8. *bhavanmaya* p. 33-34; N. 132
9. *vārdhuṣi* p. 35; N. 137
10. *sāttvatāṃ patiḥ* p. 36; N. 140
11. *nibhālaya* p. 45; N. 175
12. *hosye* p. 43; N. 167

Solutions to some of these cases were given by Bhaṭṭoji and some other writers on grammar, which are not known and not easily available to many readers. He has collected these from different sources in some cases and presented them in one handy compendium. It is in keeping with his declaration : *nāmūlaṃ likhyate kiṃcit* (verse 12). It is a kind of source-book, and in some cases is more than that as the author supplies his own answers.

V. *Some names of new works and authors cited in the S.K.U.*

Apart from the well-known works and poets, our author mentions some new names, which are not known — as far as I can search — from other sources.

1. He quotes a part of verse from one *Bhṛguvaṃśa* (p. 56).

2. He quotes from one *Rāmavijaya* (p. 68).

3. He refers to one *Narasiṃhacampūkāvya* (p. 46). This was probably the one attributed to Sūryakavi. See S. K. De, *H.S.P.*, p. 262. See also Note 177.

4. He quotes a verse from one *Raghūttamakāvya* (p. 61), which is attributed to his (elder) brother.

5. There is a reference to one *Lāvaṇyalaharī* (p. 50).

6. He quotes the last foot of a verse (*prabhus tu* etc. p. 54) which is found in full in the *Tattvabodhinī*. See Note 211. This verse is attributed by our author to one Ḍhakkārāmakavi. The name of Ḍhakkārāmakavi is not found in the *Tattvabodhinī*, or in other sources available to me.

7. He refers to one Akbarīya-Kālidāsa. But the verse cited in the *S.K.U.* (p. 60) is not found among the verses quoted by Haradatta Sharma in his article (on p. 484) in *the Indian Historical Quarterly* (v. X; 1934, September). But there is also some confusion because of the use of *Kavikalpalatāyām* here. See Note 231-a.

VI. The following is the list of works and authors mentioned in the *S.K.U.*

1. Akbarīya-Kālidāsa page 60
2. *Anekārthasaṃgraha* p. 9
3. Abhinanda p. 59
4. Amara pp. 8, 9, 18, 22, 35, 57, 59
5. *Udārarāghava* pp. 16, 20, 53
6. *Kavikalpalatā* p. 60
7. Kavirāja p. 35
8. Kālidāsa pp. 14, 17, 22, 24, 31, 32, 35, 36, 47, 57
9. *Kāvyakaṇṭhābharaṇa* p. 38
10. *Kāvyaprakāśa* pp. 5, 48
11. *Kāvyaprakāśakhaṇḍanakāra* p. 5
12. *Kāśikā* p. 25
13. *Kīcakavadha* p. 22
14. Kṛṣṇamiśra p. 36
15. Kaiyaṭa p. 21
16. Kaiyaṭa-haradattādi p. 8
17. *Gītagovinda* p. 12
18. *Cāndrasūtra* p. 18
19. *Caurapañcāśat* p. 5
20. *Jyotiśśāstra* p. 27
21. Ḍhakkārāmakavi p. 55
22. *Trikāṇḍaśeṣa* p. 22
23. *Durghaṭa Vṛtti* p. 21
24. *Devīmāhātmya* p. 47
25. *Dvirūpakośa* pp. 22, 59, 60, 62
26. *Nāmaliṅgānuśāsana* p. 8
27. *Nītiśāstra* p. 6
28. *Naiṣadha* pp. 8, 14
29. Nyāsakāra-haradattau p. 13
30. Parāśara p. 13

A NOTE ON

THE MANUSCRIPTS USED

The following Manuscripts were collated for the edition of the *Sāhityakaṇṭakoddhāra*, which is presented in the following pages.

1.	MS.	A — R6815	from the Govt. Oriental MSS Library, Madras.
2.	MS.	B — R2321	,, ,, ,, ,,
3.	MS.	C — R2597	,, ,, ,, ,,
4.	MS.	D — R5068	,, ,, ,, ,,
5.	MS.	E — D17901	,, ,, ,, ,,
6.	MS.	F — TR400	from the Adyar Library & Research Centre, Madras.
7.	MS.	G — 68650	,, ,, ,, ,,

Of these, I was able to get a microfilm of the MS. G. alone, and of the others I could get only the transcripts.

The MS. G (17″ × 1½″) is in Telugu script, and in a good condition. It ends with the expression : *chandovat purāṇāni bhavanti* — see the line 22 on page 62. Thus it is almost complete. It has about 18 folios (17 and one side of the 18th), with eight lines on each side, and about 70 syllables in each line. Only the side of the leaf ending the work has three lines. The writing is uniform and good. At the beginning verses from 2 to 13 are missing, (see Note 2) and at the end there is no colophon here indicating the completion of the work. MSS A and F have the colophon. See Note 239.

The work has three sections on

1. *Subanta* (i.e. nouns)
2. *Tiṅanta* (i.e. verbs), and
3. *Kṛdanta* (Participles).

Within the *Tiṅanta* portion there is a sub-section with the title : *Atha Padavyavasthā*. See Note 185.

The MSS. A and B are Paper manuscripts in *Devanāgarī* characters. MSS. C, D & E are in Palm-leaf and in Telugu characters. Manuscript F is in paper MS. in Grantha characters.

MS. A is complete, and the others are almost complete, as explained in Note 239. MS A has many mistakes. All others have a few mistakes. As I could get only the transcripts of the MSS C, D, & E, — I am unable to give any details regarding the number of leaves, lines etc. of these manuscripts.

Excepting one or two places (see for instance Note 163), on the whole the Manuscripts were good and helpful in the editing of the work.

I am grateful to the authorities of the Government Oriental Manuscripts Library, Madras, and of the Adyar Library and Research Centre, Madras, who were kind enough to supply me with the Manuscripts, the details of which are noted earlier.

University of Toronto T. Venkatacharya
September 10, 1979

श्रीः

साहित्यकण्टकोद्धारः

संसारमरुसंचारतृषितानां शरीरिणाम् ।
सुधाकादम्बिनीभूतं[1] तन्महः समुपास्महे ॥ १

ध्यात्वा यं मुनयो मनःसरसिजे संसारपाथोनिधेः
पारं यान्ति [2]जनुःसुखादिकमहानक्राहिभीमस्थितेः[3] ।
तं क्षीराब्धिशयानमम्बुजदृशं लक्ष्मीसमेतं विना
कं देवं शिरसा नमामि सततं विघ्नौघविच्छित्तये ॥ २

उमावामकायं हृताशेषमायं खलानामपायं श्रितानामुपेयम् ।
असन्नामधेयं महासामगेयं सुरेशं गिरीशं महेशं[4] तमीडे ॥ ३

मूर्ध्नि स्थितां हिमकरस्य कलां ग्रहीतुम्
[5]इच्छावतीं सरभसं [6]स्पृशतीं भ्रमेण ।
दृष्ट्वा हिमालयसुतां प्रहसन् महेशः
श्वश्श्रेयसं स वितनोतु निरन्तरं नः ॥ ४

1. Only MS. B reads : *sudhākādambinīṃ vāṇīṃ vīṇāpāṇim upāsmahe.* All other Mss. read what is given in the text. See the Introduction on the date of the author.

2. MS. D clearly reads : *janus sukhādika*-etc., of which *januḥ* stands for *janma.* Amara notes : *janur jananajanmāni*-etc.
MSS. A, C, & E read : *janās sukhādhika*-etc.
Ms. F reads : *janaḥ sukhānaka*-etc.
In MSS. B and G verses from 2 to 13 are missing.

3. MS. C seems to read : *bhīrusthiteḥ.*
MSS. D & F read : *bhīmasya te.*
Others read : *bhīmasthiteḥ.*

4. MSS. C & F read the beginning of the verse as : *umādāmakāyam.*
Others read : *umāvāmakāyam.*

5. MSS A & E read : *sarabhasaṃ pṛṣatībhrameṇa,* and ... *ca vitanotu.*
MSS. C & F read : *icchāvatīṃ saratnapṛsaṃṣat* (?) *bhrameṇa,* and ... *ca vitanotu.*
MS. D reads : *icchāvatīṃ ca vararatnam iti bhrameṇa,* and *śvaśśreuasīṃ carikarītu.*
Perhaps the reading intended was :
icchāvatīṃ sarabhasaṃ spṛśatīṃ bhrameṇa,
and ...*śvaśśreyasaṃ sa vitanotu* etc.
Amara notes :
śvaśśreyasaṃ śivaṃ bhadram kalyāṇaṃ maṅgalaṃ śubham.

6. Both the forms *spṛśatīṃ* and *spṛśantīṃ* are correct according to the rule 7.1.80.

शरच्चन्द्रकलाखण्डमण्डनायितमौलये ।
नमोऽस्तु [7]वामदेवाय [8]वामकामविघातिने ॥ ५

पीताम्बरावृतमुरस्स्थलकौस्तुभाल्य-
माणिक्यमण्डितमनर्घकिरीटदीप्तम् ।
सव्यापसव्यकमनीयकलत्रगात्रं
[9]श्रीपाण्डुरङ्गममलं शिरसा नमामि ॥ ६

[10]तुरीयममरुद्गणैर्नुतमुरीकृतास्त्रव्रजं[11]
करीशवदनं मनोमयदरीशयं भाविनाम्[12] ।
[13]भवाब्धिलहरीतरिं [14]प्रकृतिमाश्रये भासुरं
सरीसृपकरं हरप्रियतनूजमंहोहरम् ॥ ७

साहित्यशास्त्रसरसीरुहसूर्यभूतौ
श्रीवत्सगोत्रकनकाचलसानुभूतौ ।

7. MSS. A & E read : *vāmadevāya.*
MSS. D & F read *vāmavāmāya.*
MS. C is not clear.

vāmadeva is a synonym of Śiva. Amara notes :
Vāmadevo mahādevo virūpākṣas trilocanaḥ.

The expressions *vāmavāma* — may be analysed as *vāme (bhāge) vāmā yasya saḥ*. It would be a reference to *Ardhanārīśvara* form of Śiva, as His left side was taken over by Pārvatī according to mythology.

8. MSS. A & F read : *dāmakāmavighātine.*
MS. D reads : *vāmakāmavighātine.*
Some syllables are missing here in MSS C & E.

9. This is a reference to a form of Viṣṇu, also known as Viṭṭhala. See Apte under Viṭṭhala.

10. *Marudgaṇa* means *devagaṇa*. *Amarudgaṇa* here stands for the *Pramathagaṇa*. They were the demigods, who were attendants of Śiva, Bhṛṅgi, Riṭi etc. The expression seems intended to mean that the *Pramathagaṇas* eulogized Gaṇeśa to be the fourth powerful god, the three being the well-known Trimūrtis, Brahmā, Viṣṇu and Maheśa.

11. MS. F reads : *urīkṛtāstravrajam.*
MSS. A & E read : *urīkṛtāsyavrajam.*
In MS. C some syllables are missing.
Only MS. D reads : *turīyam aguṇair nutaṃ sakalabuddhisandhāyakam.*

12. The word *bhāva* has many meanings. Amara notes :
bhāvas sattāsvabhāvābhiprāyaceṣṭātmajanmasu.
So *bhāvinām* here means *janminām*, i.e. *śarīriṇām = saṃsāriṇām.*

13. Amara notes : *striyāṃ naus taraṇis tariḥ.*

14. *prakṛti* here means *pradhāna.*

श्रीवैद्यशास्त्रकथने[15] विजिताश्विनेयौ
कोनेरिविट्ठलबुधौ[16] प्रणमामि नित्यम् ॥ ८

नित्यं[17] वैद्यकशास्त्रमर्मविविधव्याख्यानदीक्षागुरुः
[17a]श्रीवत्सान्वयभूषणो यदभवत् तातस्तु नारायणः ।
माता यस्य पतिव्रताभिधमहाधर्माधिपत्यं[17b] गता
सोऽहं व्याकरणागमस्य सरसं सारं लिखाम्यद्‌भुतम् ॥ ९

ग्रन्थशिक्षाशतं[18] वीक्ष्य ग्रन्थिकानुपसेव्य च ।
साहित्यकण्टकोद्धारं नाम ग्रन्थं करोम्यहम्[18a] ॥ १०

15. Only MS. F reads *mathane*. Others read *kathane*.

This expression means that the two persons mentioned in the next line were famous for their proficiency in the *Āyurveda*, in which they surpassed, as people thought, even the Aśvinīdevas, the two physicians of the gods.

Vaidyaśāstra-kathane seems to be in the sense of "in the matter of expounding the science of medicine".

16. See the Introduction for the derivation and the significance of the names *Koneri-Viṭṭhalabudhau*.

17. MSS. A & E read the first line as :

yo nityaṃ bhuvi vaidyaśāstravividhavyākhyānadīkṣāguruḥ.

MSS. C, D, and F read what is given in the text.

17-a. *Bhūṣaṇa* is like *sūdana* in Madhusūdana. See Note 224. In his *H.C.S.L.* M. Krishnamachariar notes Madhusūdana to be the name of the author of the *S.K.U.* He does not supply the basis or the source for this information. In the Introductory verses or in the colophon the name of the author is not found. See the Introduction.

17-b. MSS. A & E read : *-dharmādhipatyaṃ gatā.*

In MSS. B & G the portion is missing. See Note 2.

MSS. C & F read : *-dharmāvadhitvam gatā.*

Only MS. D reads: *-dharmāvatī saṃgatā*. On the basis of the reading in the MS. D (i.e. R. 5068) the volume 6 of the *Triennial Catalogue of Sanskrit MSS* in the Oriental (MSS.) Library, Madras, contains a note mentioning Dharmāvatī as the name of the mother of the author of the *S.K.U.* The long *ā* in *Dharmāvatī* can probably be explained as in, and on the analogy of, Padmāvatī, though I have not seen that expression elsewhere. It is difficult to analyse the compound form here, and also to explain the significance of *saṃgatā*. Though none of the readings in this context indicates any poetic skill on the part of the author, I prefer *dharmādhipatyaṃ* to the others. I doubt whether we can explain any grades with reference to *pativratādharma*, and call one as the *avadhi* thereof. *Adhipati* may be in the sense of "protector" (of the *pativratādharma*). I am unable to accept Dharmāvatī as the name of the mother of our author. See the Introduction.

18. MS. E reads : *granthaśikṣāpadaṃ vīkṣya.*

MS. A reads : *granthaśikṣāpaṭuṃ vīkṣya.*

MSS. C, D, & F read what is given in the text.

[18b]न क्षुण्णोऽयं परैर्मार्गस्तत्र संचरतो मम ।
पदे पदे प्रस्खलतः सन्तः सन्त्ववलम्बनम् ॥ ११

[19]नामूलं लिख्यते किंचिन्नानपेक्षितमेव च ।
अतोऽभिलषितार्थोऽयमहेयः सहसा बुधैः ॥ १२

दूषणान्येव कुर्वन्तु किं तु दोषान् निरूप्य वै ।
फणिभाषितभाष्यज्ञा मद्ग्रन्थस्य निरन्तरम् ॥ १३

तत्रादौ सन्ध्यसन्ध्यनुसारेण उदाहरणान्युच्यन्ते ।

तद्दर्शनाय विविधा [19a]द्विजराजनार्यो
नानाविधाश्च विबुधा अपि बाहुजाश्च ।
[20]वैश्यास्तथेतरजना नृपसेवकाश्च[21]
[22]अभ्याययु र्द्रुततरं विधिना विमुक्तम् ॥ (पूर्वपीठिका-६६)

See the Introduction for the similarity of this verse and verse I.5 of the *Kavikalpalatā* of Deveśvara.

18-a. See the Introduction for a discussion about the name of the author of the *S.K.U.*, his father and ancestors.

18-b. See item III in the Introduction.

19. All the solutions to some of the linguistic problems offered by our author in this work are based on standard works in Sanskrit grammar. These are all scattered. A good deal of labour and intelligence were expended by our author in extracting the necessary answers from the scattered mines of useful information. Our author had succeeded in his efforts to a great extent. The readers will be delighted in our author's treatment of grammar "as an applied science" and not as a fundamental science (as some theoreticians would). The readers will also be glad to know about a number of puzzling usages culled from the works of well-known poets, and the interesting answers. See the Introduction.

19-a. This is the 69th verse *pūrvapīṭhikā* according to the Northern reading. The printed edn. (Poona O.S.no. 86; 1946) has the reading as : *dvijarājayas tāḥ*. All the MSS. of *S.K.U.* read *dvijarājanāryo.*

20. The printed edition reads :
vaiśyāś ca sevakajanāḥ.

What is given in the text is the reading in the MSS. of the *S.K.U.*

21. The printed edn. reads :
...nṛpasevakāś cety anye
pradudruvur aho vidhir evam uktvā.

The MSS. of the *S.K.U.* read what is given in the text, (without *iti* and without *sandhi*).

22. This verse is quoted by our author as an illustration for the absence of *sandhi* between two uncompounded words in metric lines, where *sandhi* is regarded as compulsory (*nitya*, excepting at the end of the half) by Vāmana, Mammaṭa, and others who counted the *sandhyabhāva* to be a *doṣa* known as *visandhi*.

इति (तथा) सौदामिनी[23] लसति किं जलदे प्रयाते[24]
अस्तंगते[25] शशिनि तिष्ठति चन्द्रिका किम् । (पूर्वपीठि-५३)

इति च [25a]चौरपञ्चाशति बिल्हणः ।

राजन् विभान्ति भवतश्चरितानि [26]तानि
इन्दोर्द्युतिं दधति यानि रसातलेऽन्तः ।
धीदोर्बले अतितते उचितानुवृत्ती
आतन्वती विजयसंपदमेत्य भातः ॥

इति काव्यप्रकाशे (सप्तमोल्लासे उद्धृतम्) ।

हे [26a]रोहिणि त्वमसि शीलवतीषु धन्या
एनं निवारय पतिं सखि दुर्विनीतम् ।

23. This is the 53rd verse in the same *pūrvapīṭhikā*, where the printed edn. reads *bhavati*, instead of *lasati* found in the MSS. of the *S.K.U*.

24. This verse is also quoted for the same illustration of the violation of *sandhi*, which is considered compulsory.

25. The printed edn. here also as in the previous verse (See Note 21) reads : *prayāte hy astaṃgate*, inserting *hi* in the middle. It appears to be a device adopted to avoid the difficulty of *sandhi*. It is not clear what was the original reading, if it was by Bilhaṇa.

25-a. Our author does not use the word *Caurapañcāśikā*. He uses the word *Caurapañcāśat*, and sometimes *Caurapañcāśatiya*.

26. This verse is cited in the *Kāvyaprakāśa* as an illustration for the two types of *visandhi-doṣa*, of which one is

(I) the *aicchikasandhyabhāva* based on the dictum *vākye tu sā* (*saṃhitā*) *vivakṣām apekṣate*; and the other

(II) *pragṛhyādihetukasandhyabhāva*, depending upon the rules *Īdūdeddvi-vacanaṃ pragṛhyam* (1.1.11) and *Plutapragṛhyā aci nityam* (6.1.125).

In the first case the non-application of a *sandhi* even once (*sakṛd api*) between words in each half of a verse is considered a fault, according to the poetic convention though grammatically it is not wrong.

In the second, adopting *sandhyabhāva* more than once (*asakṛt*) simply because it is permitted by express grammatical rules, is also counted to be a fault. Both these points were first noted by Daṇḍin thus :

na saṃhitāṃ vivakṣāmīty asandhānaṃ padeṣu yat,
tad visandhīti vikhyātaṃ, na pragṛhyādihetukam. (*Kāvyādarśa* III.159)

In IV.27 of his *Kāvyālaṃkāra* Bhāmaha gives an example of the second type alone, without defining the *doṣa*, and he does not illustrate the first type. Perhaps *aicchikasandhyabhāva* was not considered to be a *doṣa* by him. Later writers followed Daṇḍin. Mammaṭa also says :

saṃhitāṃ na karomīti svecchayā sakṛd api doṣaḥ.
pragṛhyādihetukatve tv asakṛt. (p. 333, Jhalakikar edn., 1965)

26-a. This verse (*he rohiṇi* etc.) is also quoted in the *Durghaṭavṛtti* under 2.4.34, and this was probably the source for Bhaṭṭoji.

जालान्तरेण मम वासगृहं प्रविश्य
श्रोणीतटं स्पृशति किं कुलधर्म एषः ॥

इति शब्दकौस्तुभे (चौखम्बा-मुद्रिते—१९३३ संवत्सरे-३१ पुटे)।

[27]वरं पितुः परीक्षेत मातुः कन्यां परीक्षयेत्।
तृणाद् भूमिं परीक्षेत आचारेण कुलं यथा ॥ इति नीतिशास्त्रे।

अत्र [28]इको यणचीत्यादिसूत्रेण सन्धिप्राप्तिरिति चेत्।
सत्यम्। प्रमादा एवैते इति जीर्णाः[29]। [30]नवीनास्तु

27. MS. E reads : *varaṃ pitā parīkṣeta* and *mātā kanyām* etc.
MS. F is not clear.
Others read what is given in the text.

28. The author seems to be having in mind Bhaṭṭoji's *Siddhāntakaumudī*, where *Iko yaṇ aci* (6.1.77) is the first rule in the *Sandhi-prakaraṇa*, whereas in the *Aṣṭādhyāyī* order *Che ca* (6.1.73) comes earlier. Our author seems to have great regards for Bhaṭṭoji. See Notes 35 and 99. In the example *tāni*+ *indoḥ* (quoted in the context) the rule *Akaḥ savarṇe dīrghaḥ* (6.1.101) is applicable.

29. *Jīrṇāḥ* perhaps refers to Daṇḍin with whom Vāmana, Mammaṭa and others agreed in the matter of the *visandhi-doṣa*.

Vāmana notes *Nityā saṃhitā ekapadavat pādeṣv ardhāntavarjam* (K.A.S.; V.I.2). As remarked in Note 26, *Aicchikasandhyabhāva* was not approved by Daṇḍin in metrical lines. This is what is mentioned by Vāmana as *nityā saṃhitā pādeṣu* etc. Majority of writers like Bhoja, Mammaṭa, Vidyānātha and a host of others record this poetic convention with their approval.

30. It is not clear who are meant by *navīnās tu*. As pointed out in Note 26, *aicchikasandhyabhāva* was not considered to be a *doṣa* by Bhāmaha. There was probably a view among the writers on Sanskrit poetics, which did not regard *saṃhitā* as compulsory (*nityā*) in metrical lines. These writers perhaps permitted absence of any *sandhi* in a verse as in a prose line, and counted it to be *correct* according to the *vivakṣā* of a poet. In the verses of well-known poets, we come across cases of absence of *sandhi*. See for instance,

soḍhuṃ na tatpūrvam avarṇam īśe
ālānikaṃ sthāṇum iva dvipendraḥ. (*Raghu*. XIV.38)

This one was cited in the *Mukhabhūṣaṇa* too (p.1). Those who held the *sandhyabhāva* to be correct do not seem to be in majority. The view of Daṇḍin seems to have gained the majority of followers. After Daṇḍin as there was no recorded evidence of the *sandhyabhāva-sādhutvavāda*, the view which was supposed to have been accepted silently by Bhāmaha, Daṇḍin's view of the *asādhutva* of the *sandhyabhāva* probably came down as "*the old view*". It seems, therefore, that the adherents of this view were referred to as *jīrṇāḥ*.

The other view, though probably was originally an earlier view, was thought to be *later view*, because of the lack of recorded statement. The followers of this view seem to be noted, therefore, as *navīnās tu*. In fact Māṇikyacandra (1160 A.D.) in his *Saṃketa* on the *K.P.*, commenting on the verse *rājan vibhānti* etc. says thus :

संहितैकपदे नित्या नित्या धातूपसर्गयोः ।
नित्या समासे वाक्ये तु सा विवक्षामपेक्षते[31] ॥

इति न्यायेन सन्धिर्नास्तीत्याहुः । [32]काव्यप्रकाशखण्डनकारास्तु इदमेव हृदि निधाय सन्धेर्वैरूप्यं नाम दोषं निराकुर्युः ।

अथ कथम्

स्फुटोत्पलाभ्याममलिदम्पतीव तद्-
विलोचनाभ्यां कुचकुड्मलाशया ।

vivakṣitaś ca sandhir bhavati (na tu avivakṣitaḥ) ityuktyāśrayaṇe tāni+indor ityatra sandhyabhāvaḥ aduṣṭa eva. (p. 143; *Ānandāśrama*, 1921)

This remark shows that in the days of Māṇikyacandra, *aicchikasandhyabhāva* was accepted to be correct by some writers. Śaraṇadeva in his *Durghaṭavṛtti* on 6.1.87 says thus :

> *ekapade'pi saṃhitā anityā* etc. *tathā ca rakṣitenoktam saṃhitaikapade nityā ityādi prāyikam iti.*

Maitreyarakṣita probably belonged to the beginning of the 12th century. Similarly Nāgeśa in his commentary on the *Kāvyaprakāśa-pradīpa* notes : *aicchikasandhyabhāvasya khedādinā vicchidya pāṭhe na duṣṭatvam iti kecit. yathā ekā ekā śiroruhā* iti. The *ādi* in *khedādinā* deserves attention. It is thus clear that even in the days of Nāgeśa, there were some who accepted the *aicchikasandhyabhāva* even in verse to be *correct*. The author of the *S.K.U.* has in mind these writers, who seem to be referred to as *navīnās tu*.

31. This *kārikā* (*saṃhitaikapade* etc.) is attributed to Bhartṛhari in the *Bālamanoramā*. See *Siddhāntakaumudī* on *Śeṣe vibhāṣā* etc. (8.4.18). But the *kārikā* is not found in the available *Vākyapadīya*. Bhaṭṭoji in his *Śabdakaustubha* says about *saṃhitaikapade* etc. thus :

> *iyaṃ prācāṃ paribhāṣā ekadeśānumatidvārā saṃhitādhikāreṇaiva jñāpitā. asaṃhitāyaṃ yaṇādinivṛttyartho hi saṃhitādhikāraḥ.*
>
> (*Ibid.* on *A I U Ṇ*; p. 31)

This remark seems to imply that the dictum *saṃhitaikapade* etc. was very ancient and that it was in existence even before Pāṇini, who approved of its acceptability by means of his governing rule *Saṃhitāyām* (6.1.72).

32. It does not seem to be a reference to Siddhicandra, the author of the *Kāvyaprakāśakhaṇḍana*, as S. C. counts the *aicchikasandhyabhāva* to be a *doṣa* (see pp. 38-39; K. P. Kh.).

S. C. simply says (after the *K. P.*) thus :

> *saṃhitāṃ na karomīti svecchayā sakṛd api doṣaḥ. pragṛhyādihetuke tu asakṛt.* (p. 39).

It may be a reference to Śrīvatsalāñcchana, who in his *Kāvyāmṛta* (S.V. U.O Series 1,1971; p. 31) rejects the *visandhi-doṣa* along with *upahatalupta-visarga*, and *hatavṛtta*. He does not use the words *aicchikasandhyabhāvo na doṣaḥ*. He does not quote the line : *sā vivakṣām apekṣate*. But he says *eteṣāṃ guṇābhāva-rūpatvam eva, na doṣatvam*. Śrīvatsalāñcchana was earlier than Jagannātha*. See the Introduction on the date of the author of the *S.K.U.*

निपत्य बिन्दू हृदि कज्जलाविलौ
मणीव नीलौ तरलौ विरेजतुः ॥ (नैषधचरिते ६-८५)

इति नवमे श्रीहर्षः । अत्र मणी इवेति पदच्छेदे ईदूदेद्द्विवचनं प्रगृह्यम् (१-१-११) इति प्रगृह्यसंज्ञा स्यात् । (ततश्च प्लुतप्रगृह्या अचि नित्यम् (६-१-२५) इति सूत्रविहितेन प्रकृतिभावेन भवितव्यम्) इति चेत् ।

अत्र केचित् [33]मणीवादे र्नेति निषेधात् प्रगृह्यसंज्ञा नास्तीत्याहुः । तत् [34]मुनित्रयानुक्तत्वाद् अप्रमाणमिति कैयटहरदत्तादयः । वस्तुतस्तु मणी व इति पदभेदे इवार्थकेन वशब्देन व्याख्याने न कश्चित् पूर्वपक्षावसरः इति [35]भाष्यरहस्यज्ञाः । तथाच—अमरः[36]—व वा यथा तथेवैवम् साम्ये इति ।

अत्र केचित्[37] वद् वा इति पाठम् (अमरवाक्ये) इच्छन्ति । तदयुक्तम् । नामलिङ्गानुशासने [38]प्रातिपदिकप्रक्रमे तद्धितस्य वतेः अननुगुणत्वात् । अपत्यसमूहादि-पर्यायमध्ये अण्[39]-फिञ्-वुञादीनामनुक्तेश्च । तथा च हेमचन्द्रः—

33. The *Kāśikāvṛtti* (on 1.1.11) notes :
ivādīnāṃ pragṛhyatve maṇīvādīnāṃ pratiṣedho vaktavyaḥ. maṇīva, dampatīva, rodasīva.

Nārāyaṇa, the commentator on the Naiṣadha, quotes this prohibitive statement from the *Kāśikā*, and explains the usage. Our author is perhaps referring here to Nārāyaṇa.

34. Bhaṭṭoji gives the same line in his *Śabdakaustubha*, and the *Prauḍhamanoramā* (....*apramāṇam iti kaiyaṭādayaḥ*). See the next Note.

35. This is a reference to Bhaṭṭoji, See also Notes 99, and 119, and the text connected therewith. Bhaṭṭoji also quotes the verse *sphuṭotpalābhyām* of the *Naiṣadha* (S.K., Vol. I. p. 127).

36. This Amara was quoted by Bhaṭṭoji too.

37. Kṣirasvāmin in his commentary on the Amara, and (following him perhaps) Liṅgayasūri, the author of the *Amarapadavivṛti* (also known as *Liṅgābhaṭṭīyam*) have the reading :
vad vā yathā tathā etc.

38. Bhaṭṭoji says in his *Śabdakaustubha* :
yuktaś cāyam eva (va vā iti) pāṭhaḥ. prātipadikaprakrame taddhitasya vater ananuguṇatvāt.

39. This is a reference to the *Taddhita* (secondary) suffixes prescribed by the rules such as (1) *Śivādibhyo'ṇ* (4.1.112); *śivasyāpatyaṃ śaivaḥ*; (2) *Tikādibhyaḥ phiñ* (4.1.154); *tikasyāpatyaṃ taikāyaniḥ*; (3) *Tasya samūhaḥ* etc.; *gotra... manuṣyājād vuñ* (4.2.37 & 39); *manuṣyāṇāṃ samūhaḥ mānuṣyakam* etc.

This reason is not found in the *Ś.K.*, but was noted by Bhaṭṭoji's son Bhānoji in his commentary *Sudhā* on the *Amara*. This is a good point utilized by our author from the *Sudhā*, though the name is not mentioned. This reason lends further support to the argument that rejects the reading *vad, vā* etc. in the *Amara*. *Vat* is a *Taddhita* suffix, which by itself cannot be used as an independent expression like *yathā, tathā*. The reading of *vat*, therefore,

[40]वः पश्चिमदिगीशे स्याद् वौपम्ये पुनरव्ययम् इति ।

(अनेकार्थसंग्रहे—१-१५)

अथ कथम्

कटो ना श्रोणिफलकं कटिः श्रोणिः ककुद्मती—इत्यमरः ।
दृप्तः ककुद्मानिव चित्रकूटः—(रघुवंशे १३-४७) इति रघुश्च ।
ककुद्मान् इत्यत्र प्रत्यये भाषायां नित्यम् इत्यनेन (८-४-४५ इत्यत्रत्येन वार्तिकेन) नित्यमनुनासिकप्राप्तेरितिचेत् । अत्राहुः—मादुपधायाश्च मतो र्वोऽयवादिभ्यः (८-२-९) इतिसूत्रस्थयवादिगणे[41] (ककुद्) इति दकारान्तत्वेन पाठात् सर्वापेक्षया [42]गणपाठस्य बलीयस्त्वादिति ।

here cannot be an authentic and correct one. To support the point Bhānoji (and following him our author also) says that Amara does not use other *Taddhita* suffixes such as *aṇ*, *phiñ*, *vuñ* etc. while giving the synonyms of *apatya* and of *samūha*. See Amara :

ātmajas tanayas sūnur apatyaṃ tokam etc., and *samūho nivaha*-etc., where these suffixes are not included.

40. In his *Anekārthasaṃgraha* Hemacandra has the following :

vaḥ paścimadigīśe syāt vaupamye punar avyayam (I.15).

From the words *aupamye punar avyayam* it appears that Hemacandra means that *va* (with short *a*) as a particle of similitude is indeclinable, whereas in the sense of Varuṇa *va* is declinable in masculine gender (*vaḥ*). This style is adopted by him to bring out the contrast between an *avyaya* in one sense and an *anavyaya* in another. He says later :

a syād abhāve svalpārthe viṣṇāv eṣa tv anavyayam (7.1)

The line of Hemacandra (on *va*) is similar to the line *Medinī*, which reads :

vaṃ pracetasi jānīyād ivārthe ca tad avyayam.

This *Medinī* is quoted by *Bālamanoramā* (on 1.1.11) too.

41. Bhaṭṭoji gives this answer in his *S. K.* (under *pratyaye bhāṣāyāṃ nityam*). Mallinātha also comments on *kakudmantaḥ* in *Raghu.* 4.22 as : *yavāditvād* etc.

42. In the light of Bhaṭṭoji's comment : *yavādigaṇe dakāranipātanāt* (see previous Note), the statement of our *gaṇapāṭhasya balīyastvāt* is intended to mean *gaṇe dṛṣṭasya nipātanasya balīyastvāt*. For the meaning of *nipātana* Nāgeśa says :

anyādṛśe prayoge prāpte anyādṛśaprayogakaraṇam.

(*Paribhāṣendu-*, on *Abhedakā guṇāḥ*)

(Contrary to the ordinary rules of grammar, when a specific form is noted (by Pāṇini) in a rule, it is intended to show that the specific form so noted has a greater force and thus the ordinary rules are superseded). Under *Sarvādīni sarvanāmāni* (1.1.27) Patañjali says :

bādhakāny eva nipātanāni. (See also the *Paribhāṣendu-*).

अथ कथम् [43]विश्वे देवास्त्रयो दशेति । सर्वादीनि सर्वनामानि इतिसूत्रे संज्ञोपसर्जनीभूतास्तु[44] न सर्वादयः इति निषेधात् कथं जसः[45]शीकार्यम् इति चेत्-सत्यम् । संज्ञापदार्थस्य आधुनिकपदार्थविषयत्वात् । प्रकृते तु (विश्वे देवा इत्यत्र) वेदे प्रसिद्धत्वात् । देवगणविशेषवाचकस्य विश्वशब्दस्याधुनिकसंकेताभावात् सर्वनामकार्यं भविष्यत्येवेति [46]समादधौ ।

कथं तर्हि

अधरे नववीटिकानुरागो नयने कज्जलमुज्ज्वलं दुकूलम्[47] । इति ।
(इदमाभरणं नितम्बिनीनामितरद् भूषणमङ्ग दूषणाय ।।)
अधरे विनिवेश्य वंशनालम् इति[47a] च ।

अत्र अधरशब्दस्याधुनिकसंकेताभावात् कोशादिषु च ओष्ठे प्रसिद्धत्वात् पूर्वपरावरदक्षिणोत्तरापराधराणि व्यवस्थायाम् असंज्ञायाम् इति सूत्रेण (१-१-३४) सर्वनामसंज्ञा[48] स्यादिति चेत् । उच्यते । तत्र व्यवस्थायामिति नियमात् । प्रकृते तु दक्षिणा गाथकाः । प्रवीणा इत्यर्थः इतीव प्रत्युदाहरणत्वेन व्यवस्थायाः[49] अभावेन सर्वनामसंज्ञा न भवतीति ।

43. "Name of a particular group of deities" Apte.

44. See *S. K.* under 1.1.29, where this is given as *vārttika* in the printed edition. This is based on the *vārttika Saṃjñopasarjanapratiṣedhaḥ*, and the relevant discussion in the *Mahābhāṣya* under 1.1.27. See also *Nyāsa* & *Padamañjarī* on 1.1.27.

45. According to the rule *Jasaś śī* (7.1.17) the basic suffix (*jas*) is replaced by *śī* in the case of pronouns. Of the *śī* only *ī* remains in practical use. Thus *sarva*+*ī* - *sarve*. In the case of ordinary nouns, i.e. *rāma*+*as*=*rāmāḥ*.

46. This seems to be a reference to Bhaṭṭoji. He says in his *Prauḍhamanoramā* (under *Pūrvaparāvara*-etc. p. 439; Chowkhamba edn; 1939) thus :

ādhunikasaṃketo hi saṃjñā; etena viśveṣāṃ devānām iti vyākhyātam. vedaprasiddhatvāt. devagaṇaviśeṣe viśva-śabdasya ādhunika-saṃketābhāvāt.

47. The second half of the verse is not given by the author. (Source not known).

47a. The example *adhare viniveśya* etc. is found in the margin only in MS. G.

48. The point of the question is this : The word *adhara* is also to be counted as a *sarvanāman*, according to the rule 1.1.34. Consequently, in the locative case, by applying the pronominal termination *smin* (7.1.15) the expression must be *adharasmin*, and not *adhare*. For the answer see the next Note.

49. The rule *Pūrvaparāvara*-etc. (1.1.34) records that the words listed therein were regarded as *sarvanāman*, if the words in the context were relative terms. For instance see *pūrva*=eastern with reference to some thing; *dakṣiṇa*=southern with reference to some point. Or they should be

अथ कथम्—

अत्यर्थमुद्वेजयिता परेषां[50] नाम्नापि तस्यैव स नन्वकोऽभूत् (३-१६)

इति माघः ।

अत्र परशब्दस्य कोशादिषु शत्रौ प्रसिद्धत्वात् (अधरशब्दे इव व्यवस्थायाः अभावे) कथं सर्वनामकार्यम् इति चेत्—

अत्राहुः । देशवाचितया व्यवस्थाविषयत्वात् (सर्वनामसंज्ञकस्य) तस्यैव परशब्दस्योपचाराच्च शत्रौ प्रयोगः । न च (एवं सति) उपसर्जनतया (संज्ञोपसर्जनीभूतास्तु न सर्वादय इत्यनेन सर्वनामसंज्ञायाः) निषेधः (स्यात्) इति वाच्यम् । न हि लाक्षणिकत्वमुपसर्जनत्वम् । किं तु स्वार्थविशिष्टार्थान्तरवत्त्वम् ।

comparative terms, such as *uttara*=upper; *adhara*=lower (than the other etc.). This is the meaning of the rider *vyavasthāyām*, (which is explained as *svābhidheyāpekṣāvadhiniyamo vyavasthā*). The word *adhara* is not strictly a relative term, in the sense of lower lip, because it is regarded as a synonym of "lip" in general. The lexicographer Halāyudha notes thus :

adharo radanacchada oṣṭha ucyate,
dantavāsaś ca (II.369).

Consequently when the word *dakṣiṇa* is used in the sense of a skilled person in general, it is not counted as a Pronoun. Similarly *adhara* is a synonym of *oṣṭha* in general, as is held by some, whom Bhaṭṭoji and our author seem to follow. As a result the word *adhara* is not a Pronoun, and therefore is not eligible for the pronominal termination. In the examples such as *adhare tāmbūlarāgaḥ* (given by Bhaṭṭoji in *P. M.*, p. 439) and *adhare navavīṭikānurāgaḥ*, the word *adhara* need not mean lower lip alone, as the *tāmbūlarāga* is seen on the upper lip also. This is the answer to the question raised in this context. See the previous Note also. Bhaṭṭoji mentions the counter example *uttare pratyuttare ca śaktaḥ* too.

50. Bhaṭṭoji gives two more usages of *para* and *apara* thus :

tathā pareṣāṃ yudhi ceti pārthivaḥ (*Raghu*-III.21)

and *apare pratyavatiṣṭhante*. The second one is a common expression met with in many works, where it is used to introduce the opinion of some who are opposed to the view previously noted in the context. *Para* in the first usage means "enemy", and *apara* means an opponent. These are not, here, in the sense of next or subsequent etc. and so are not relative terms. Thus when there is no *vyavasthā* (see previous Note), the pronominal terminations are not applicable. The *pūrvapakṣin* means that the forms should be *parāṇām* (not *pareṣām*) and *aparāḥ* (not *apare*). For similar uses having *apare* see the following :

tasyābhāvaṃ jagadur apare (*Dhvanyāloka*, I.2) and
tad apare na kṣamante (*Khaṇḍanakhaṇḍakhādya*, p.13).

तच्च समासादिवृत्तावेवेति केचित् । वस्तुतस्तु परशब्दस्य [51]देशान्तरनिष्ठत्व-मेवार्थः । शत्रुत्वादिकं तु आर्थिकोऽर्थ इति भाष्यरहस्यज्ञाः[52] ।

अथ कथम्—

लुलितचलितदृग्भिः कोपकोपाञ्चिताभिः
ललितवचनवीचीवल्लिभिर्वल्लयद्भिः[53] ।
तदपि लिखित[54]बुद्धो तत्पदासक्तचित्ते
हरि हरि हरिणाक्ष्या वीक्षणे कोऽप्युपायः ॥

इति सरस्वतीकण्ठाभरणे[55] ।

[56]हरि हरि हतादरतया गता सा कुपितेव
(गीतगोविन्दे ३-७-३)

इति गीतगोविन्दे च ।

अत्र ह्रस्वस्य गुण इति सूत्रेण (७-३-१०८) गुणप्राप्तेः इति चेत्—अत्र

51. MSS. A, C, E and F read : *deśāntaraviṣayatvam evārthaḥ*; MSS. B, D, & G read : *deśāntaraniṣṭhatvam eva-*, and this one is the recording in the *Prauḍhamanoramā* also.

52. This is a reference to Bhaṭṭoji, who has a good discussion in this context in his *P.M.* (p. 439). The arguments are reproduced here.

53. All the MSS. read the verse thus. But the meaning is not clear to me. Until we get the correct reading of the verse it may be difficult to make out the meaning. *kāmukaiḥ* or some other substantive is perhaps to be supplied, so as to be construed with *vallayadbhiḥ*.

54. It is not clear whether we should read :

tadabhilikhitabuddhau.

MSS. A & E read : *tad api lihitabuddhau.*

MSS. B, C, D, & G read *vihitabuddhau.*

55. All the MSS. note *Sarasvatīkaṇṭhābharaṇa* as the source. But I am unable to trace this verse in that work of Bhoja.

56. (1) The commentary *Samjīvanī* notes :

hari hari iti mahat kaṣṭam, and *hari hari kaṣṭe'dbhute ca iti yādavaḥ.*

I do not find this in the *Vaijayantīkośa* of Yādavaprakāśa available to me.

(2) The commentary *Jayantī* on the same says :

hari hari iti khede.

(3) The commentary *Padadyotanikā* says :

hari hari iti khedānukāre. This should be a correct approach. Though *hari hari* as such may not be a pure Sanskrit form, this was perhaps imitative of the expression of the regional language, indicating distress. The efforts of some to justify this usage according to the rules of Sanskrit grammar by twisting and elasticising them are unnecessary, and appear to be too pedantic.

वदन्ति । प्रमाद एवायमित्येके । केचित्तु श्रोर्गुण (६-४-१४६) इति ज्ञापकात् संज्ञापूर्वको विधिरनित्य[57] इति न्यायेन प्राप्तोऽपि गुणो नेति वदन्ति ।

अथ कथम्

(रामाय रामभद्राय रामचन्द्राय वेधसे ।)
रघुनाथाय नाथाय सीतायाः पतये नमः ॥ इति (रामायणे)
नष्टे मृते प्रव्रजिते क्लीबे च पतिते पतौ ।

इति पराशरश्च ।

अन्यत्र पतिना[58] सह—इति स्मृतिश्च ।

अत्र पतिः समास एव (१-४-८) इति सूत्रे एवकारेण समासे एव घिसंज्ञा न तु केवलस्येत्यर्थनियमात् प्रकृते च समासाभावात् घिसंज्ञायाः अभावे कथं (पतिना) पतये पतौ इत्यादि रूपम् इति चेत्—सत्यम् । पतिरित्याख्यातः पतिरित्याख्यातार्थण्यन्तात् टिलोपे अच इः (उणादिसूत्रम्-५७८) इत्यौणादिके इप्रत्यये रूपसिद्धिः । न च भक्षितेऽपि लशुने न शान्तो रोगः इति न्यायेन अत्रापि (पतिशब्दे) स पूर्वपक्षः संभवतीति वाच्यम् । लक्षणप्रतिपदोक्तयोः प्रतिपदोक्तस्यैव[59] ग्रहणम् इति परिभाषया प्रतिपदोक्तस्यैव ग्रहणात् । न तु लाक्षणिकस्य । पातेर्डतिः (उणादिसूत्रम्—४६७) इतिसूत्रनिष्पन्नस्य प्रतिपदोक्तत्वात् । इप्रत्ययान्तशब्दस्य लाक्षणिकत्वात् (पतिः समास एव इति) सूत्रे न ग्रहणम् । तथा च शेषो घ्यसखि (१-४-७) इति सूत्रेण घिसंज्ञायाः सत्त्वात् रूपाणामेतेषां साधुत्वम् इति समादधुः । एतेन

सखिना वानरेन्द्रेण—इति रामायणम्
कृष्णस्य सखिरर्जुनः—इति भारतं च व्याख्यातम्[60] ।

57. See the *Kāśikā* on 6.4.146, and the *S.K.* of Bhaṭṭoji. There is a difference of opinion about the *Paribhāṣā*, which is rejected by Nāgeśa. See his *Paribh.* Our author does not refer to Nāgeśa's rejection of this *Paribhāṣā*. Perhaps the *Paribhāṣenduśekhara* had not yet become known by the time of our author. See Note 205 and the Introduction on the date of the author. See also previous Note for my opinion on *hari hari*.

58. These examples : *sītāyāḥ pataye*, and *patite patau* are quoted by Bhaṭṭoji also. See his *P.M.* p. 502.

Durghaṭavṛtti gives two other examples (under 1.4.8) :

patinā nīyamānāyāḥ, and *patau jīvati yā nārī* etc.

These are also quoted in the *Amarapadapārijāta*, with a reference to *Subhutiṭikā*. See the commentary on the *Amarakośa* (Adyar Publication, p. 382).

59. See the *Paribhāṣenduśekhara* for the *paribhāṣā*.

60. This is also noted by Bhaṭṭoji (Ibid. p. 502).

अथ कथम्—

वयं कलादा इव दुर्विदग्धं त्वद्गौरिमस्पर्धि दहेम हेम ।
प्रसूननाराचशरासनेन सहैकवंशप्रभवभ्रु बभ्रु ।। (नैषधे ८-६६)

इति श्रीहर्षः । तथा

यदि तु तव समागमे तथैव प्रसरति सुभ्रु ततः कृती भवेयम् ।।

इति विक्रमोर्वशीये (३-२२) कालिदासश्च ।

सुभ्रु इत्यत्र नेयङ्वङस्थानावस्त्री (१-४-४) इति सूत्रेण [61]नदीसंज्ञानिषेधात् अम्बार्थनद्योर्ह्रस्वः (७-३-१०७) इति सूत्रेण (नदीसंज्ञकस्य विहितः) ह्रस्वः कथम् इति चेत्—सत्यम् । प्रमाद एवायमिति प्रामाणिकाः । सामान्ये नपुंसकम् इति वा कथंचित्[62] समाधेयमित्यपरे ।

अथ कथम्—

अखिलमिदममुष्य गौरीगुरोस्त्रिभुवनमपि नैति मन्ये तुलाम् ।
अधिवसति सदा यदेनं जनैरविदितविभवो [63]भवानीपतिः।।
(किरातार्जुनीये ५-२१)

61. In the rule *Aci śnudhātubhruvām* etc. (6.4.77) the word *bhrū* is noted as eligible for *uvaṅ* (i.e. *uvaṅyogya*). So the forms are *bhruvau* etc. Consequently the prohibition of *Nadīsaṃjñā* recorded in the rule *neyaṅuvaṅsthānāv astrī* (1.4.4) holds good in the case of *bhrū*. As a result the shortening of *ū* in vocative singular is a violation of the recorded prohibition. The form should have been *he subhrūḥ* (and not *subhru*) is the essence of the question. For the answer see next Note.

62. The answer is furnished by depending upon the difference of opinion about the applicability of the prohibition. This naturally involves twisting and a far-fetched interpretation of rules.

First it was started by Vāmana (see his *K.A.S.V.* on V.2.48), and it was followed by the author of the *Jayamaṅgalā* on Bhaṭṭi-*kāvya* (VI.11), Mallinātha on Bhaṭṭi and *Kumārasaṃbhava* (V.43), and the anonymous author of the *Mukhabhūṣaṇa* (p. 39; Adyar Library Pamphlet Series 41; 1973).

By applying the feminine suffix *ūṅ* to the word (though the stem is ending in long *ū* already), and thus by treating *bhrū* to be different from the original *bhrū* (that was without *ūṅ*) they explain that the rule *Aci śnu*-etc. (6.4.71) is not applicable here (perhaps by the *paribhāṣā lakṣaṇapratipadoktayoḥ pratipadoktasya grahaṇam*). As a result, the *subhrū* being not *uvaṅsthāna*, the prohibition (1.4.4) is avoided. Thus becoming *nadīsaṃjñaka*, the shortening rule *Ambārthanadyoḥ* etc. (7.3.107) reigns supreme. Hence the form *subhru* in vocative singular. For further details, see *Kāmadhenu* on *K.A.S.V.* (V. 2.48), and *Jayamaṅgalā* and Mallinātha referred to above. This far-fetched interpretation is not echoed by Bhaṭṭoji and some others. Our author simply seems to follow Bhaṭṭoji. See his *S.K.*, *P.M.* (p. 552) and *Tattvabodhinī* after the rule 4.1.5.

63. See also (1) Murāri IV.23, (2) the verse *na trastam* etc. in Act II.28 of the *Mahāvīracarita*, (3) the *Mālatīmādhava* after verse IX.3, and the *Kādambarī* p. 295 (Mathurānātha śastri edn. N.S.P.).

इति भारविः । अत्र भवस्य स्त्रीति विग्रहे पुंयोगादाख्यायामिति सूत्रेण (४-१-४८) ङीषि इन्द्रवरुणेत्यादिसूत्रेण (४-१-४९) आनुकि च कृते भवानीपदेनैव ईश्वरोपस्थितौ पतिशब्देन पुनस्तस्याः पत्यन्तरोपस्थितिः स्यात् इति चेत्— सत्यम् । प्रमाद एवायमित्यालंकारिकाः[64] । (शिवा भवानी रुद्राणी इत्यादि-कोशात् भवानीशब्दस्य गौरीपर्यायतया योगरूढ्या संज्ञात्वेनैव पार्वतीवाचकत्वम् । तेन उमापति शब्दस्येव) भवानीपतिशब्दस्य ईश्वरवाचकत्वेन न दोष[65] इत्येके ।

अथ कथम्—

कुवलयदलनीला कोकिला बालचूते इति ।

(वामनस्य काव्यालंकारसूत्रवृत्तावुदाहृतमिदम् ५-२-४६)

तरुणभुजगनीला सैव वेणी तदेत-

च्छ्रवणयुगमनङ्गन्यस्तडोलाद्वयाभम् । ( )

इति महावीरचरिते च ?

अत्र हि जानपदेतिसूत्रेण (४-१-४२) विहितस्य ङीषो वा संज्ञायामिति वार्तिकेण संज्ञायामेवेति विकल्पनियमात् नीलादोषधौ प्राणिनि चेति वार्तिकरीत्या ङीष् स्यात् (ततश्च नीली इति रूपेण भवितव्यम्) इति चेत्—सत्यम् । प्रमाद एवायमिति [66]प्रामाणिकाः ।

अथ कथम्—

उपर्युपरि बुद्धीनां चरन्तीश्वरबुद्धयः इति ।

(आर्यशूरस्य जातकमालायाम्)

अत्र आम्रेडितयोगे बुद्धीनामित्यत्र

उभसर्वतसोः कार्या धिगुपर्यादिषु त्रिषु ।

द्वितीयाम्रेडितान्तेषु ततोऽन्यत्रापि दृश्यते ।। इति वार्तिकोरीत्या

(१-४-४८) द्वितीयाप्राप्तेरिति चेत्—सत्यम् । अत्र उपर्युपरीति नाम्रेडितम् । किं तु उत्तानबुद्धीनाम् उपरि ईश्वरबुद्धयश्चरन्तीति व्याख्येयम् इत्याहुः[67] ।

64. See the *K.P.* the verse *na trastam* etc. quoted in the 7th chapter as an example of *viruddhamatikṛt*.

65. See Pūrṇasarasvati on the word Bhavānīpati in the *Mālatīmādhava* after verse IX. 3 (pp. 497-498, TSS).

66. See Vāmana's K.A.S. V. 2.46 and the *Vṛtti* thereon.

67. The verse from the *Jātakamālā* of *Āryaśūra* was quoted by Vāmana in his K.A.S.V. (V.2.84). *Durghaṭavṛtti* explains *uparibuddhīnām* (*bahuvrīhi*) as *uttaralabuddhīnām*, (II.3.2; p. 45). Bhaṭṭoji who also quotes this in his *P.M.* (p. 872) explains the word as *uttānabuddhīnām*, and this is reproduced by our author. The *sāmīpya-dvirvacana* by the rule 8.1.7 is regarded as the one that governs the dvitiyā, according to the *paribhāṣā lakṣaṇapratipadoktayoḥ* etc. Instead of having the *sāmīpyadvirvacana*, by having recourse to the

अथ कथम्—

भेजेऽभितः पातुकसिद्धसिन्धोरभूतपूर्वा [68]श्रियमम्बुराशेः

(माघे—३-३)

अत्र अभित इत्यनेन योगे [69]पातुकसिद्धसिन्धोरित्यत्र अभितः परितः (२-३-२ सूत्रे) इत्यादिवार्तिकरीत्या द्वितीयाप्राप्तेरिति चेत्—अत्राहुः। तस्मिन्नेव वार्तिके (अभितः परितः समयानिकषा-हा-प्रति-योगेष्वपि—इति) अपि[70]शब्दाद् (द्वितीयायाः विकल्पसिद्धया) अत्र द्वितीया न भवतीति। एतेन

हा[71] राम हा राघव हा कुमार हा वत्स हा वत्सल मत्समीपम् (उदारराघवे-४-८१) इत्युदारराघवे (प्रयुञ्जानः) शाकल्यमल्लो व्याख्यातः।

vīpsādvirvacana, the application of the *dvitīyā* is thus avoided by Vāmana, Bhaṭṭoji and others. See *P.M.* : *atra...vīpsāyāṃ kṛtadvitvasya na grahaṇam* etc. (p. 872). The *Śabdaratna* quotes also this :

sarveṣām ayam (or *agham*?) *amlānām uparyupari vartate* and notes thus : *atra hyuparyuparītyasya atiśayo'rtho*; *na sāmīpyam. vīpsāyām cātra dvirvacanam.* (Ibid.)

68. According to Mallinātha, *rucam* is the reading instead of *śriyam.*

69. The word *abhitaḥ* has two meanings: *ubhayataḥ* and *abhimukham* (i.e. "around" and "near"—literally "in front of"). Vallabha and Mallinātha take it in the sense of *ubhayataḥ*. Further, instead of having it as a separate word, they explain it as a part of compound word (i.e. *abhitaḥpātukā*= *ubhayataḥpātinī* etc.). Our author seems to take it in the sense of *abhimukha*, and as an uncompounded word. This could govern *dvitīyā* on *siddhasindhu* (meaning "near the celestial river"). The expanded sentence would be : *pātukasiddhasindhoḥ abhimukhaṃ* (or—*sindhum abhitaḥ*) *tiṣṭhataḥ amburāśeḥ śriyaṃ sa hariḥ bheje.* Regarding *abhitaḥ* in the sense of *abhimukha* see Mallinātha on *Kirātārjunīya* II.59, where *gurum abhitaḥ* is explained as *guror abhimukham* etc. Also see *Nipātāvyayopasargavṛtti* (p. 27; S.V.O.I., 1951). *Āyāntam abhitaḥ kāntam* is the usage quoted in this context. It is not clear whether the meaning of *abhimukha* was noted by some commentators on the Māgha (III.3). Haradatta notes on II.3.2 : *ābhimukhyavṛttir api...abhitaśśabdo'sti. so'pi gṛhyate.*

70. The *Nyāsakāra* notes here thus :

> *apiśabdo vikalpārthaḥ. api dṛśyate dvitīyā*; *api na dṛśyate ca. tena hā tāta hā mātar ityādi siddhyanti* (2.3.2)

In the *Hanumannāṭaka* occurs : *hā tāta hā mātaḥ* (III.5)

It is not clear from where the *Nyāsakāra* is quoting the line. Also see H.N.IV.14, V.8 & 9. Kaiyaṭa and Haradatta however note thus :

> *hā kanye ityādau kārakavibhaktitvād ... antaraṅgatvāt sambodhanavibhaktir bhavati* (II.3.2)

Our author seems to follow the *Nyāsakāra*.

71. See also the previous Note and similar usages quoted therein. See also *Udārarā*.I.68; I.100; & IV.66.

अथ कथम्—

तत्रागारं धनपतिगृहादुत्तरेणास्मदीयम् (मेघसंदेशे २-८)

इति कालिदासः। अत्र उत्तरेणेत्येनप्प्रत्ययान्तयोगे धनपतिगृहादित्यत्र एनपा द्वितीया (२-३-३१ इति सूत्रेण द्वितीयाप्राप्तेरिति चेत्—न। नायमेनप्प्रत्ययान्तः। किं तु तृतीयान्तः। उत्तरेण तोरणेनेत्यन्वय [72]इत्याहुः।

ननु कथम्—

[73]तुलां यदारोहति दन्तवाससा इति (कुमारसंभवे—५-३४)

कालिदासः।

स्फुटोपमं भूतिसितेन शंभुना इति (शिशुपालवधे १-४)

माघश्च। अत्र तुल्यार्थैरतुलोपमाभ्यां तृतीयान्यतरस्याम् (२-३-७२) इति सूत्रेण (अतुलोपमाभ्यामिति निषेधात्) तृतीयायाः अप्राप्तत्वात्। अत्र तुलोपमाशब्दयोरेव प्रयोगात् इति चेत्—उच्यते। अत्र सहयुक्तेऽप्रधाने (२-३-१९) इति तृतीया। (सहशब्दप्रयोगाभावेऽपि तदर्थे गम्ये तस्याःसाधुत्वात्।) उक्तं हि विनापि तद्योगं तृतीया[74] (सिद्धान्तकौमुद्याम्) इति।

यथा—

स्ववालभारस्य तदुत्तमाङ्गजैः स्वयं चमर्येव तुलाभिलाषिणः (नैषधे १-२५)

श्रीहर्षप्रयोगे।

अथ कथम्—

प्रभुर्बुभूषुर्भुवनत्रयस्य यः शिरोऽतिरागाद्दशमं चिकर्तिषुः (माघे १-४९)

इति माघः। अत्र नमः स्वस्तीति सूत्रेण (२-३-१६) चतुर्थी स्यात्। तस्मै प्रभवतीति ज्ञापकात् अलमिति पर्याप्त्यर्थग्रहणमिति व्याख्यानात्[75]। तेन प्रभुशब्दयोगे चतुर्थी युक्तेति कथं भुवनत्रयस्येति षष्ठी—इति चेत्—सत्यम्। स एषां ग्रामणीः (५-२-७८) इति सूत्रकारनिर्देशात् प्रभ्वादियोगे षष्ठ्यपि साधुरिति समा[76]दधुः।

72. Mallinātha also notes this as an alternate interpretation. Perhaps by *āhuḥ* our author is referring to Mallinātha.

73. Also see the *Raghuvaṃśa* : (VIII.15)

nabhasā nibhṛtendunā tulām uditārkeṇa samāruroha tat.

74. See also the *Kāśikā* on 2.3.19. Haradatta, Mallinātha, Bhaṭṭoji and others explain the *tṛtīyā* with *tulā* and *upamā* in a different manner. See *Padamañjarī* on 2.3.72 and Mallinātha on *Raghu*-VIII.15, on *Māgha* I.4, and *Kumāra*—V.34.

75. See the *Kāśikā* on 2.3.16, and the *S.K.* on the same.

76. This is a reference to Bhaṭṭoji. See his *S.K.* on 2.3.16, and the *Mahābhāṣya* under 2.3.16, which is the source for others.

अथ कथम्—

स्रक् पारिजातस्य ऋते नलाशां वासैरशेषामपुपूरदाशाम् (नैषधे ६-८६)

इति श्रीहर्षः ।

न मामृते राम रमेत वाली । इति च ।

को हि लब्ध्वा प्रियान् पुत्राञ्छपेदेवं पितामह ।

ऋते कद्रूं तीक्ष्णरूपां देवदेव तवाग्रतः ॥

इति माहाभारते आदिपर्वणि जरत्कारूपाख्याने । अत्र अन्यारादितरर्ते—(२-३-२९) इत्यादिसूत्रेण ऋते नालशामित्यादौ पञ्चमी स्यादिति चेत्—अत्राहुः । प्रमाद एवायमित्येके । अन्ये [77]तु—उभसर्वतसोरित्यत्र (ततोऽन्यत्रापि दृश्यते इति) दृशिग्रहणात् ऋते-योगे द्वितीयापि साधुरित्याहुः । युक्तं चैतत् । ऋते द्वितीया च इति चान्द्रसूत्रात् ।

अथ कथम्—

कुमार्य इव कान्तस्य त्रस्यन्ति स्पृह्यन्ति च । इति ।

अत्र कान्तस्येत्यत्र त्रसियोगे भीत्रार्थानां भयहेतुः (१-४-२५) इतिसूत्रेण (अपादानसंज्ञायाम्) पञ्चमीप्राप्तेः । तथा स्पृहियोगे स्पृहेरीप्सितः (१-४-३६) इति सूत्रेण (संप्रदानसंज्ञायाम्) चतुर्थीप्राप्तेश्चेति चेत्—अत्राहुः[78] उभयत्रापि शेषत्वविवक्षायां षष्ठीति ।

अथ कथम्—

कस्य बिभ्यति देवाश्च जातरोषस्य संयुगे ।

इति रामायणम् । अत्र बिभेतेर्योगे भीत्रार्थानां भयहेतुः (१-४-२४) इति सूत्रेण (अपादानसंज्ञायाम्) संयुगे इत्यत्र पञ्चमीप्राप्तेरिति चेत्—अत्र [79]वदन्ति । कस्य संयुगे इत्यन्वयात् परया अधिकरणसंज्ञया बाधात् इति ।

अथ कथम्—

मणिबन्धादाकनिष्ठं करस्य करभो बहिः

इत्यमरः । अत्र अपपरिबहिरञ्चवः पञ्चम्या (२-१-१२) इतिसमासविधान-[80]ज्ञापकात् बहिर्योगे करस्येत्यत्र पञ्चमीप्राप्तेरिति चेत्—अत्राहुः ज्ञापकसिद्धं न सर्वत्रेति [81]परिभाषया तदभावसिद्धिः ।

77. This is a reference to Bhaṭṭoji. See his *P.M.* (p. 927).

78. This is again a reference to Bhaṭṭoji. See his *S.K.* on 1.4.36. He has similar discussion in the *Śabdakaustubha* too, on 1.4.36.

79. See *P.M.* (p. 923).

80. See the *Kāśikā* on 2.1.2.

81. See the Durghaṭavṛtti (2.1.12) and the *Paribhāṣenduśekhara* for the *paribhāṣā*.

अथ कथम्—

स्मरत्यदो दाशरथिर्भवन् भवानमुं वनान्ताद् वनितापहाररिणम् (१-६८)

इति माघः।

मुहुरनुस्मरयन्तमनुक्षपं त्रिपुरदाहमुमापतिसेविनः । (५-१४)

इति भारविश्च। अत्रादः स्मरतीत्यन्वये अधीगर्थदयेशां कर्मणीति सूत्रेण (२-३-५२) स्मृत्यर्थधातुयोगे षष्ठी यात्। यथा वा

सस्मार वारणपतिः परिमीलिताक्षमिच्छाविहारवनवासमहोत्सवानाम् (५-५०)

इत्यत्र माघे । इति चेत्—

अत्राहुः—अधीगर्थेतिसूत्रे कर्मणः शेषत्वविवक्षायामेव षष्ठीतिव्याख्यानात् प्रकृते च शेषत्वस्य अविवक्षणाद् द्वितीयेति।

अथ कथम्—

अपि वागधिपस्य दुर्वचं वचनं तद् विदधीत विस्मयम् (२-२)

इति भारविः।

इक्ष्वाकूणां दुरापेऽर्थे त्वदधीना हि सिद्धयः (१-७२)

इति रघुवंशे च। अत्र दुर्वचमिति दुरापे इति च खलर्थयोगेन न लोकाव्यय-निष्ठाखलर्थतृनाम् (२-३-६९) इति षष्ठीनिषेधात् कथं वागधिपस्येति इक्ष्वाकूणा-मिति च प्रयोगः साधुः स्यात् इति चेत्—अत्र वदन्ति। निषेधसूत्रस्य [82]कारकषष्ठी-विषयत्वात् षष्ठी शेषे (२-३-५०) इति सूत्रेण विहिता या षष्ठी सा तु स्यादेवेति। अन्ये तु [83]इक्ष्वाकूणां सिद्धय इति वागधिपस्य विस्मयमिति चान्वये खलर्थ-योगाभावात् न कश्चिद् दोष इति समादधुः।

अथ कथम्

अतिशयान्ध्यवपुः क्षयपाण्डुताः स्मर भवन्ति भवन्तमुपासितुः (नैषधे ४-८५)

इति श्रीहर्षे। अत्र उपासितुरिति तृजन्तयोगे भवन्तमित्यत्र कर्तृकर्मणोः कृति (२-३-६५) सूत्रेण कर्मणि षष्ठी स्यादिति चेत्—सत्यम्। नायं तृजन्तः। किं तु तृन्नन्तः। तत्र न लोकेति (२-२३-६९) षष्ठीनिषेधात् कर्मणि द्वितीयेति समादधुः।

82. See Ś.K. on 2.3.69, and the S.K. where this point is discussed.

83. This is given as an alternate explanation by Mallinātha on *Kirāta* II.2, and Bhṭṭoji in his Ś.K. on 2.3.69 in this context.

अथ कथम्—

[84]अधिमत् कृते सुमुखि भाषितेन किम्

इत्युदारराघवे शाकल्यमल्लः । अत्र (हरौ इत्यधिहरि-इतिवत्) मयि इत्यर्थे (अव्ययं विभक्तीति-२-१-६) अव्ययीभावसमासे शेषे लोप इतिसूत्रेण (७-२-९०) दकारलोपे नाव्ययीभवादतोऽम्त्वपञ्चम्या इतिसूत्रेण (२-४-८३) अमादेशे (अमिपूर्व इति (६-१-१०७) इति पूर्वरूपे) अधिमम् इति स्यात् मध्ये-युवं गच्छतु मैथिलीतिवत् । इति चेत्—अत्राहुः—प्रमाद एवायमिति बहवः । संज्ञापूर्वको विधिरनित्य इति न्यायेन शेषे लोप इति न दकारलोपः लोपसंज्ञापूर्वकत्वात् । तथा च अदन्तत्वाभावात् अमादेशो नेति वयं पर्यालोचयामः[85] ।

अथ कथम् —

(हठादाकृष्टानां कतिपयपदानां रचयिता
जनः स्पर्धालुश्चेदहह कविना वश्यवचसा ।)
[86]भवेदद्य श्वो वा नियतमधुना पापिनि कलौ
घटानां निर्मातुस्त्रिभुवनविधातुश्च कलहः ॥ इति ।

(भोजचरित्रे २४८)

84. So far I have not been able to verify and find out the exact reading. MS A. reads : *ayi matkṛte.*
MS. E reads simply : *matkṛte.*

Others read clearly *adhimat.* The discussion in the context seems to imply *adhimat* to be the reading. *kṛte, matkṛte, yatkṛte, tatkṛte* etc. are different expressions. See Śabdakaustubha on 2.2.11,(p. 220, where some of these are quoted and discussed.

adhimat and *kṛte* (locative absolute) are separate expressions. *Adhimat* seems to be in the sense of "about me" or "to me" or "towards me". In the absence of the context, I am unable to make out the full meaning intended. What I am mentioning is only my guess. The line seems to mean "(Something) having (already) been done about me or to me, what is the use of talking now ?" In verse III.31 (*muniveṣadambhayuji* etc.) *adhimat* is used by Sākalyamalla, and it seems to be in the same sense.

85. The author would, similarly, regard as correct the usages like *adhitvat* (=*tvayi*), *adhyasmat* (=*asmāsu*), *adhiyuṣmat* (=*yuṣmāsu*), *adhiyvam* (=*yuvayoḥ*), *adhyāvam* (*āvayoḥ*). But I have not seen any of these usages.

86. Only MS. B has a discussion here on the use of *dṛśām* in the verse *ādāvañjanapuñja-etc.*, which is found in other MSS. later (see p. 44). This MS. (B) has the discussion on *tribhuvanavidhātuḥ*, after discussing the *dṛśām.*

अत्र कर्मणि षष्ठ्याः [87]तृजकाभ्यां कर्तरि (२-२-१५) इति सूत्रेण षष्ठी-समासनिषेधात् घटानां निर्मातुरितिवत् त्रिभुवनस्य विधातुरित्यसमस्तेन भवितव्यम्। तेन कथं समास इति चेत्—

सत्यम्। प्रमाद एवायमिति बहवः। कैयटस्तु तृजकाभ्यां कर्तरि (२-२-१५) कर्तरि च (२-२-१६) इत्यादिषष्ठीसमासनिषेधस्य सूत्रान्तरविहितषष्ठीविषयत्वात् षष्ठी शेषे (२-३-५०) इति सूत्रेण विहिता या षष्ठी तया सह षष्ठी (२-२-८) इतिसूत्रेण (राज्ञः पुरुषो राजपुरुष इतिवत्) समासे बाधकाभावादित्यभिप्रायेण शेषषष्ठ्या[88] समास इति [89]समादधौ। अथ वा नात्र षष्ठीसमासः। किं तु द्वितीयेति (२-१-२४) योगविभागाद् त्रिभुवनविधातेति द्वितीयासमास इति दुर्घटवृत्तिकारः (२-२-१६)। न[90] च विधातेति कृत्प्रत्ययान्तशब्दप्रयोगे कर्तृकर्मणोः कृतीति (२-३-६५) कर्मणि षष्ठ्येव स्यात्। ततश्च तृजकाभ्यामित्यादिषष्ठीसमासनिषेधो वज्रलेपायत इति वाच्यम्। तदर्हमिति (५-१-११७) सूत्रज्ञापकात् कर्तृकर्मणोः कृतीति (२-३-६५) षष्ठ्याः अनित्यत्वात्[91]। तथा च षष्ठीप्राप्त्यभावे समासनिषेधस्य दूरमपास्तत्वात् गर्जन् द्वितीयासमासो भविष्यतीति यदन्यैरेवोक्तं तद् युक्तमिति वयमालोचयामः।

87. The MS. G reads *kartarīti sūtreṇa*, and I think that the rule here is *tṛjakābhyāṃ kartari* (2.2.15). All other MSS. read *karmaṇi ca*, which does not seem to be correct. There was some confusion in the understanding of the rules *Tṛjakābhyām* (2.2.15) and *Kartari ca* (2.2.16). For a clear interpretation, see the *P.M.*, and the *Śabdakaustubha.*

88. Commenting on the expression *guṇiviśeṣaka* in the *Mahābhāṣya* under 1.4.21, Kaiyaṭa says thus :

> *ata eva vacanād anityaḥ ṣaṣṭhīsamāsapratiṣedhaḥ.*
> *śeṣaṣaṣṭhyā vā samāsaḥ.* (p. 236; Vol. II.N.S.P.)

See also the *Nyāsa* and the *Padamañjarī* on 4.1.33 on *phalagrahītṛtvāt*, and on 2.2.12 (*janikartuḥ tatprayojaka ityādau śeṣaṣaṣṭhyaiva samāsasya siddhatvāt*).

These are mentioned by Bhaṭṭoji in his *Ś.K.* under 2.2.15.

89. See also the *Nyāsa*, which says :

> *tena—bhīṣmaḥ kurūṇāṃ bhayaśokahartā* (*Mahābhārata*?)
> *ityādi siddhaṃ bhavati.*

The *Nyāsakāra* justifies the expression by having the *tṛn* suffix (instead of the usual *tṛc*). He however seems to imply about the first element that it would be case of *śeṣe ṣaṣṭhī.*

90. In MSS. A & G *na ca* is missing. Others have it.

91. See the *P.M.*, and the *Ś.K.* on 2.3.65, and the *Jayamaṅgalā* and Mallinātha on Bhaṭṭi VI.79 (or 80)—(*dhāyair āmodam*).

अथ कथम्—

तान्युच्छषष्ठाङ्कितसैकतानि (रघुवंशे ५-८)

इति कालिदासः। अत्र उच्छानां षष्ठः इति विग्रहे पूरणगुणेति (२-२-११) सूत्रेण समासनिषेधापत्तिरिति चेत् —सत्यम्। प्रमाद एवायमित्येके। उच्छेषु षष्ठः उच्छात्मकः षष्ठः –इत्यादि[92] रीत्या वा व्याख्येयम्।

अथ कथम्—

व्यध्वो दुरध्वो विपथः कदध्वा कापथः समाः

इत्यमरः। व्यध्वे विपथकापथौ इति रभसकोशश्च। अत्र विगतः पन्थाः कुत्सितः पन्थाः इति विग्रहे कुगतिप्रादयः (२-२-१८) इति समासे ऋक्पूरब्धूः पथामानक्षे (५-४-७४) इति सूत्रेण (अ-इति) समासान्तप्रत्यये पथः संख्याव्ययादेः (स नपुंसकम् इतिसूत्रवृत्तौ सि-कौमुद्यां स्थितेन) इति वार्त्तिकेन क्लीबता स्यात्। अस्तु क्लीबत्वमिति चेत्। विपथं कदध्वा [93]कापथं समाः इति पाठस्त्वपेक्षितः स्यात्। तथा च नैकशेषो न संकरः इति (कोशादौ निर्दिष्टस्य) मूलकारनियमस्य भङ्गापत्तेः इति चेत्—अत्राहुः। प्रमाद एवायमिति बहवः। वस्तुतस्तु पथे गतो इति धातोः पचाद्यचि (३-१-१३४) पथति व्याप्नोतीति पथः इत्यकारान्तोऽयम्। तथा च समासे पुंस्त्वप्रयोगः साधुरेवेति। अत एव त्रिकाण्डशेषः—वाटः पथश्च मार्गः स्यात् इति। [93a]द्विरूपकोशोऽपि त्वचि त्वचः किरोऽपि स्यात् किरा प्रोक्तः पथः पथि इति।

ननु विपथसिद्धावपि कापथसिद्धिः कथम्। कादेशस्य दुर्लभत्वात् इति चेत्—सत्यम्। ईषदर्थे[94] च (६-३-१०५) इतिसूत्रेण तत्संभवात्। कुत्सायामर्थतः पर्यवसानात्।

अथ कथम्—

[94a]नृपतिसभामगमन्नवेऽपमाने इति कीचकवधे (२-२५)

अत्र सभा राजा अमनुष्यपूर्वा (२-४-२३) इति सूत्रे (राज-) पर्यायस्यैवेष्यते इति वार्त्तिकेण क्लीबत्वप्राप्तेरिति चेत्—सत्यम्। गजपतिवद् राजविशेषवाचित्वात् इति[95] समादधुः।

92. See also Mallinātha on *Raghu*-V.8, and Vāmana's *K.A.S.* V.1.17.

93. See the *Durghaṭavṛtti* on 2.4.30. Bhaṭṭoji says that Kṣirasvāmin and *Durghaṭavṛtti* suggested this emendation into neuter form. See *Ś.K.* on 2.4.18.

93-a. *Dvirūpakośa* is not mentioned by Bhaṭṭoji.

94. See the *Ś.K.* on 2.4.18.

94-a. The *Kīcakavadha* (of Nitivarman) was edited by S. K. De (1929).

95. See the *Durghaṭavṛtti* on 2.4.23, and also the *Ś.K.* This was quoted therein as the view of Rakṣita (i.e. Maitreyarakṣita). Some other justifications are also suggested in these texts (q.v.).

अथ कथम्--

इक्षुच्छायानिषादिन्यस्तस्य गोप्तुर्गुणोदयम् ।
आकुमारकथोद्घातं शालिगोप्यो जगुर्यशः ।। (रघुवंशे ४-२०)

इति कालिदासः । अत्र इक्षूणां छायेति विग्रहे छाया बाहुल्ये (२-४-२२) इति सूत्रेण नपुंसकत्वप्राप्तेरिति चेत्--अत्राहुः । इक्षुच्छाये आ समन्तात निषादिन्य इत्याङ[96]प्रश्लेषो बोध्यः इति ।

अथ कथम्---

(छादितः कथमपि त्रपयान्तर्यः प्रियं प्रति चिराय रमण्याः ।)
वारुणीमदविशङ्कमथाविश्चक्षुषोऽभवदसाविव रागः ।।
(माघे १०-१६)

इति माघः ।

(पृथुदर्विभृतस्ततः फणीन्द्रा विषमाशीर्भिरनारतं वमन्तः)।
अभवन् युगपद् विलोलजिह्वायुगलीढोभयसृक्कमाविः ।। (माघे २०-४२)

इति च ।

अत्र आविश्शब्दस्य साक्षात्प्रभृतिषु (१-४-७४) पाठात् विभाषा कृञि (१-४-७२) इति सूत्रस्यानुवृत्त्या साक्षात् प्रभृतीनि चेति सूत्रेण कृञो योगे एव (आविशब्दस्य) गतिसंज्ञाविकल्पः । भ्वस्तियोगे तु (भूधातोरस्तेश्च योगे तु) ऊर्यादिच्विडाचश्च (१-४-६१) इति सूत्रेण नित्यमेव गतिसंज्ञा स्यात् । ततश्च ते प्राग् धातोः (१-४-८०) इति नियमात् भूधातुना योगे आविश्शब्दस्य अव्यवहितपूर्वप्रयोग एव युक्तः । प्रकृते तु व्यवहितप्रयोगात् परतया प्रयोगाच्च दोषः इति चेत्---सत्यम् । प्रमाद एवायमिति वृत्तिकारादीनां मतेन गम्यते । निरङ्कुशाः कवयः[97] इति हरदत्तः । वस्तुतस्तु ते प्राग्धातोः (१-४-८०) इतिसूत्रस्य [98]प्रयोगनियमार्थत्वपक्षे प्रकृतेऽनुपपत्तावपि संज्ञानियमार्थत्वपक्षे दोषलेशोऽपि नास्तीति

96. See the *Ś.K.* on 2.4.22.

97. The wording here is the same as was used by Bhaṭṭoji.
See his *Ś.K.* on 1.4.61.
It is Haradatta who quotes these usages to illustrate the question. The wording of his answer is *svatantrāḥ kavayaḥ*. See *op. cit.* Mallinātha on *Māgha* X.19 says :

āvirbhuvor vyavadhānaṃ kavisvātantryāt.

98. See the *Ś.K.* on 1.4.61 for the two interpretations of *prayoganiyama* and *saṃjñāniyama*. Our author is referring to Bhaṭṭoji by *Bhāṣyarahasyajñāḥ*.

[99]भाष्यरहस्यज्ञाः। अत एव छन्दसि परेऽपि (१-४-८१) व्यवहिताश्च (१-४-८२) इतिसूत्रद्वयस्य व्यर्थतामापादयामास भगवान् भाष्यकारः[100]।

अथ कथम्—

अपशङ्क मङ्क परिवर्तनोचिताश्चलिताः पुरः पतिमुपेतुमात्मजाः।
(अनुरोदितीव करुणेन पत्रिणां विरुतेन वत्सलतयैष निम्नगाः)॥
(४-४७)

इति माघः। पुरः पतिम् इत्यत्र पुरोऽव्ययम् (१-४-६७) इतिसूत्रेण गतिसंज्ञायां नमस्पुरसोर्गत्योः (८-३-४०) इतिसूत्रेण सत्वप्राप्तेरिति चेत्—अत्र पुरः स्थितं पतिमिति स्थितपदाध्याहारेण योजनायां पतिं प्रत्यगतित्वादिति[101]। एतेन

अमुं पुरः पश्यसि देवदारुं पुत्रीकृतोऽसौ वृषभध्वजेन।
(यो हेमकुम्भस्तननिस्सृतानां स्कन्दस्य मातुः पयसां रसज्ञः॥)
(रघु-२-३६)

इति प्रयोगोऽपि व्याख्यातः।

ननु

सा दक्षरोषात् सुदती ससर्ज (कुमारसंभवे १-५३)

इति कालिदासप्रयोगः

सुदतीजनमज्जनार्पितैर्घुसृणैर्यत्र कषायिताशया (नैषधे २-७७)

इति श्रीहर्षप्रयोगश्च कथं संगच्छते। अत्र शोभना दन्ता यस्या इति बहुव्रीहौ सुदन्तीति स्यात्। न च वयसि दन्तस्य दतृ (५-४-१४१) इतिसूत्रेण दत्रादेशो भविष्यतीति वाच्यम्। (प्रथमोदाहरणे देवतात्वेन वयोविशेषानवगमः। (द्वितीयेऽपि) स्त्रीमात्रं प्रतीयते। न तु वयः इति चेत्—अत्र वदन्ति। (वामनोक्तरीत्या[102] सुदत्यादीनां योगरूढशब्दत्वेन) स्त्रियां संज्ञायाम् (५-४-१४३) इति दत्रादेशे सिद्धिः। सर्वत्र स्त्रीमात्रं विवक्षितम्। तेन शोभना दन्ताः अस्याः समस्ता जाताः न तु न्यूनाः इत्यर्थात् कथं चिद् वयोऽवगम्यते इति वा व्याख्येयम्।

99. See also Notes 35 & 119.

100. Bhaṭṭoji in his *Ś.K.* (1.4.61) quotes the uses of *sukaṭaṃkarāṇi vīraṇāni* and *svāḍhyaṃbhavaṃ* from the *Mahābhāṣya* 1.4.80 and 3.3.127 respectively in order to illustrate the correctness of the *vyavahitaprayoga*. (The uses are not *kaṭaṃsukarāṇi* or *āḍhyaṃsubhavam*).

101. The *Tattvabodhinī* says under *Puro'vyayam* (1.4.67) thus :
Amuṃ puraḥ paśyasi devadārum (*Raghu* I.36)
ityatra tu sthitamity adhyāhāreṇa dṛśiṃ pratyagatitvāt satvābhāvaḥ.
This was in the *P.M.* too.

102. See Vāmana's *K.A.S.* V.2.66 and the *vṛtti* thereon, and Nārāyaṇa and Mallinātha on *Naiṣadha* II.77, and *P.M.* on 5.4.141.

अथ कथम्—

विनसा हतबान्धवा (भट्टिकाव्ये ५-८)

इति भट्टिः । अत्र विगता नासिका यस्याः इति बहुव्रीहौ वेर्ग्रो वक्तव्यः इति ख्यश्च इति च वार्त्तिकद्वयेन (उपसर्गादनोत्पर इतिसूत्रव्याख्याने कौमुद्यां दृश्यताम्) ग्रादे-शख्यादेशयोरन्यतरेण भवितव्यम् । ततश्च कथं विनसेति चेत्—सत्यम् । विगतया नासिकया उपलक्षितेति (तत्पुरुषसमासमाश्रित्य) कथञ्चिद् व्याख्येयमिति समादधुः[103] ।

अथ कथम्—

स्वलावण्याशंसाधृतधनुषमह्नाय[104] तृणवत् (महिम्नस्तवे -२३)

इति पुष्पदन्तः । अत्र धनुषश्चेतिसूत्रेण (५-४-१३२) अनङ्प्राप्तेः (धृत-धन्वानम् इतिरूपेण भवितव्यम्) इति चेत्—सत्यम् । अत्र समासान्तविधेर-नित्यत्वादिति समादधुः[105] ।

ननु कथम्—

प्रजा इवाङ्गादरविन्दनाभेः शंभोर्जटाजूटतटादिवापः

(माघकाव्ये ३-६५)

इति माघः । अच्प्रत्यन्ववेति सूत्रे (५-४-७५) अच् इति योगविभागात् अन्यत्रापि दृश्यते पद्मनाभः ऊर्णनाभः इतिकाशिकोक्तरीत्या अत्राप्यच्प्रत्यय-प्राप्तेरिति चेत् अत्राहुः । समासान्तविधेरनित्यत्वमिति समाधानं कृतप्रायमेवेति । इदं तु विचार्यते । अरविन्दाकारा नाभिर्यस्येति विग्रहे गौणेनारविन्दशब्देन सामानाधिकरण्याद् अस्तु समस्तपदमदन्तम् इदन्तं वा । अरविन्दं नाभौ यस्येति विग्रहे तु सप्तमीविशेषणे बहुव्रीहौ (२-२-३५) इतिसूत्रेण नाभिशब्दस्य पूर्व-निपातापत्तेरिति चेत्—अत्र वदन्ति । गड्वादिभ्यः परा सप्तमी वाच्या (२-२-३५

103. See *Jayamaṅgalā* on Bhaṭṭi V.8. Mallinātha explains it in a different way. Bhaṭṭoji follows *Jayamaṅgalā*. See the *Ś.K.* on *Upasargād anotparaḥ* (8.4.28).

104. See Vāmana's *K.A.S.* V.2.65 and the *Vṛtti* thereon.

See the *Harṣacarita*

dhṛtadhanuṣi bāhuśālini śailā na namanti yat tad āścaryam

(VII. in the beginning)

See *Uttararāmacarita* V.4, and Bhaṭṭi I.24.

The verse from the *Mahimnastava* was quoted in the *Durghaṭavṛtti* and *P.M.* too under 5.4.132.

105. See *Durghaṭavṛtti* & *P.M.* and the *Tattvabodhinī* (5.4.132). This answer was given in these works.

इतिसूत्रसंबद्धेन) इति वार्त्तिकेण परनिपातसिद्धिः । नाभिशब्दस्य गड्वादित्वं कल्पनीयमिति[106] ।

अथ कथम्—

जनयति कुमुदभ्रान्ति धूर्तबको बालमत्स्यानाम्

इति । अत्र पोटायुवतीतिसूत्रेण (२-१-६५) धूर्तशब्दस्य परनिपात एव स्यात्—इति चेत्—प्रमाद एवायमिति –प्रामाणिकानां[107] पन्थाः ।

अथ कथम्—

कनकभङ्ग पिशङ्ग दलैर्दधे सरजसारुणकेसरचारुभिः ।
(प्रियविमानितमानवतीरुषां निरसनैरसनैरवृथार्थता ॥) (६-४७)

इति माघः

सरजसमकरन्दनिर्भरासु प्रसवविभूतिषु भूरुहां विरक्तः । (७-४२)

इति च ।

सरजसमपहाय केतकीनाम् (किरातार्जुनीये १०-२६) इति भारविश्च ।

अचतुरेति सूत्रे (५-४-७७) साकल्यार्थाव्ययीभाव एव सरजसमिति निपात्यते इति नियमात् । प्रकृते च बहुव्रीहिसमाससत्त्वात् सरजस्कमिति भाव्यम् । कथं सरजसमिति प्रयोग इति चेत्—प्रमाद एवायमिति [108]प्रामाणिकाः । केचित् तु महाकविप्रयोगप्राचुर्यदर्शनात् अव्ययीभावदर्शनं प्रायिकमिति पक्षाश्रयणाद् बहुव्रीह्यर्थोऽपि साधुरेवेति समादधुः[109] ।

अथ कथम्—

स सौष्ठवौदार्यविशेषशालिनीं विनिश्चितार्थामिति वाचमाददे ।
(किरातार्जुनीये १-३)

106. See *P.M.* and *Tattvabodhinī* on *Padmanābha* quoted under *Ac pratyanvava*—etc. (5.4.75).

107. See *S.K.* on 2.1.65. The *Durghaṭavṛtti* notes here :
vyaktiparo'tra bakaśabda iti kaścit.

108. See Vāmana's *K.A.S.V.*2.63 and the *Vṛtti* thereon. See the *Mahābhāṣya*, *Kāśikā*, and the *Śabdakaustubha* on 5.4.77.

109. This seems to be a reference to Mallinātha, who on Māgha VI.47 says thus :

na sarajasam ity anavyayībhāve iti vāmanaḥ.
atha vā mahākaviprayogaprācuryadarśanād
avyayībhāvadarśanaṃ prāyikam iti pakṣaśrayaṇād
bahuvrīhyartho'pi sādhur eva.

This alternate explanation does not seem to have been noted by others. This was not noted even in the *Mukhabhūṣaṇa.* See also Note 113.

इति भारविः ।

लोचनाधरकृताहृतरागा वासितानन विशेषितगन्धा

(किरात ९-६०)

इति च । अत्र सौष्ठवं चौदार्यं चेति लोचने चाधरश्चेति चोभयत्रापि द्वन्द्वे श्रौदार्याधरशब्दयोः अजाद्यदन्तम् (२-२-३३) इतिसूत्रेण पूर्वनिपातापत्तेरिति चेत्— अत्राहुः । अनित्यमिदं पूर्वनिपातप्रकरणम् । लक्षणहेत्वोः क्रियायाः (३-२-१२६) इतिसूत्रे अल्पाचोऽपि हेतुशब्दस्य पूर्वनिपातमकुर्वता सूत्रकारेण तथा[110] ज्ञापनादिति । एतेन

सस्ने माघमघातिघाति यमुनागङ्गौघयोगे यया (नैषधे १५-८९)

इति श्रीहर्षः पञ्चत्र्येकमिता दिवाकरगुणा अङ्काः कति स्युर्वद

इति ज्योतिश्शास्त्रं च व्याख्यातम् ।

अथ कथम्—

शिरःपृष्ठोरसां मूलमालस्यं भिन्नवर्णता

इति वाग्भटः । छिन्नेषु भिन्नेषु पाणिपादेषु इति च । अत्र द्वन्द्वे कृते द्वन्द्वश्च प्राणितूर्यसेनाङ्गानाम् (२-४-२) इतिसूत्रेण नित्यमेकवद्भावः स्यादिति चेत्— अत्रोच्यते । मुखनासिकावचनोऽनुनासिकः (१-१-८) इतिसूत्रे मुखं च नासिका चेति भाष्यकारोक्तपक्षाज्ज्ञापकादस्य (एकवद्भावस्य) [111]अनित्यत्वमिति । नासिकास्तनयोर्ध्माधेटोः (३-२-२९) इति सूत्रकारनिर्देशादपि तथेति वयम् ।

अथ कथम्—

रञ्जिता नु विविधास्तरुशैला नामितं नु गगनं स्थगितं नु

(किरातार्जुनीये ९-१५)

इति प्रयोगः । अत्र तरवश्च शैलाश्चेति—द्वन्द्वे जातिरप्राणिनाम् (२-४-६) इतिसूत्रेणैकवद्भावप्राप्तेरिति चेत्—सत्यम् । नायं द्वन्द्वसमासः । किं तु तरुसहिताः शैला इति शाकपार्थिवादिसमास इति समादधुः[112] ।

110. See Mallinātha on *Kirāta* I.3, where he quotes the *Kāśikā* also from 3.2.126. See the *Nyāsa* and *Padamañjarī* on 3.2.126, which mention also the uses : *dhūmāgnī*, and *mṛdaṅgaśaṅkhapāṇavāḥ* etc. See also *Kāśikā* on 4.4.118. See also *P.M.* on 2.2.33.

111. Patañjali notes the view also :

sarvo dvandvo vibhāṣayaikavad bhavati

under 1.2.63, and on 2.4.12. The *Nyāsakāra* on 1.2.63 refers to this line as a *paribhāṣā*.

112. See *Ś.K.* on 2.4.6.

अथ कथम्—

येनापविद्धसलिलस्फुटनागसद्मा देवासुरैरमृतमम्बुनिधिर्ममन्थे

(किरात-५-३०) इति भारविः। अत्र देवाश्चासुराश्चेति द्वन्द्वे येषां च विरोधः शाश्वतिकः (२-४-९) इतिसूत्रेण एकवद्भावः स्यादिति चेत्—अत्राहुः। एतेषां कार्यार्थ एव विरोधो न गोव्याघ्रादिवत्[113] शाश्वतिक इति।

अथ कथम्—

भयस्य पूर्वावतरस्तरस्विना मनस्सु येन द्युसदां न्यधीयत

(माघकाव्ये १-४३)

इति माघः। द्युसदामित्यत्र तत्पुरुषे कृति बहुलम् (६-३-१४) इतिसूत्रेण आदितेया दिविषदः (अमरकोशे) इत्यत्रेव अलुगापत्तेरिति चेत्—सत्यम्। अस्मिन्नेव सूत्रे बहुलग्रहणात् अलुक् न भवतीत्याहुः।

ननु—

जनार्दनस्त्वात्मचतुर्थ एव (महाभाष्ये ६-३-५ इत्यत्रोद्धृतमिदम्) इति कथं संगच्छते। अत्र आत्मनापञ्चमः आत्मनादशमः इतिवत् आत्मनश्च (६-३-६) इति पूरणे इति वक्तव्यम् इति च सूत्रवार्त्तिकाभ्यां तृतीयायाः अलुगापत्तेरिति चेत्—अत्र वदन्ति (भाष्यकाराः) नायं तृतीयासमासः। किं तु आत्मा चतुर्थो यस्येति बहुव्रीहिरिति। न चात्राप्यलुक् स्यादिति भ्रमितव्यम्। सूत्रवार्त्तिकयोः तृतीयासामालुग्विषयत्वात्।

अथ कथम्—

पौरोहित्यं रजनिचरितं ग्रामणीत्वं नियोगो
माठापत्यं वितथवचनं साक्षिवादः परान्नम्।
ब्रह्मद्वेषः खलजनरतिः प्राणिनां निर्दयत्वं
मा भूदेवं मम पशुपते जन्मजन्मान्तरेऽपि॥

इति प्रयोगः। अत्र मठपतिशब्दात् दित्यदित्येत्यादिसूत्रेण (४-१-८५) प्राग्दीव्यतीयेष्वर्थेषु ण्यप्रत्यये तद्धितेष्वचामादेः (७-२-११७) इत्यनेन वृद्धौ माठपत्यमिति स्यात् इति चेत्—प्रामादिकमेवेदमिति बहवः। आङ्प्रश्लेषेण वा कथंचित् निर्वाहः कार्य इति केचित्।

113. See Mallinātha on *Kirāta* V.30, from where this is quoted. See Note 109.

The *Śabdakaustubha* on 2.4.9 says thus :

teṣāṃ hi amṛtādiprayuktaḥ kādācitko virodho na tu nityaḥ. manthanapravṛttikāle tadvirahāt.

Durghaṭavṛtti on 2.4.9 has this :

devānām asurāṇāṃ ca kādācitko virodha iti rakṣitaḥ.

अथ कथम्——

(सुवर्णपुङ्खाः सुदृढाः सुतीक्ष्णा वज्रोपमा वायुसमानवेगाः ।
यावन्न गृह्णन्ति शिरांसि बाणाः) प्रदीयतां दाशरथाय मैथिली ।।

(हनुमन्नाटके ७-८)

इति प्रयोगः । अत्र दशरथस्यापत्यमिति विग्रहे अत इञ् (४-१-९५) इति सूत्रेण इञ्प्रत्ययप्राप्तेः (दाशरथये इति भवितव्यम्) इति चेत्——अत्राहुः ।[114] अपत्यरूपविशेषस्याविवक्षायां शैषिकोऽण्प्रत्ययो भविष्यतीति ।

अथ कथम्——

दाक्षायणीमुखसरोरुहकर्णिकायाम् इति ।
दाक्षायणी श्रीरिव निर्बभासे इति च ।

अत्र दक्षस्य साक्षादपत्यं स्त्रीति विग्रहे अत इञि (४-१-९५) इतिसूत्रेण इञि दाक्षिरिति स्यात्——इति चेत्——अत्र दक्षस्यापत्यं दाक्षायणीति अपत्ये गोत्रत्वोपचारात् गोत्रे कुञ्जादिभ्यः (४-१-९८) इतिसूत्रेण च्फञ् प्रत्यये जातेरस्त्रीविषयादयोपधात् (४-१-६३) इति ङीषि च स्त्रीप्रत्यये [115]रूपमित्याहुः । अन्ये तु दक्षस्यापत्यं दाक्षिः । अत इञ् (४-१-९५) । ततः आसुरेरुपसंख्यानम् वार्त्तिके (४-१-१९ सूत्रस्थे) आसुरि-दाक्ष्योरुपसंख्यानमित्युपसंख्यानाद्[116] दाक्षायणीति भवतीति वदन्ति । अपरे तु दक्षम् अयते प्राप्नोतीति विग्रहे अय गताविति धातोः ल्युटि प्रज्ञादित्वात्[117] (५-४३८) अणि रूपमित्याहुः ।

वस्तुतस्तु दक्षस्यापत्यं स्त्री दाक्षिः । ततो वा नामधेयस्य वृद्धसंज्ञा वाच्या[118] इति वार्त्तिकेण वृद्धसंज्ञायाम् उदीचां वृद्धादगोत्रात्(४-१-१५७) इतिसूत्रेण फिञ् इति प्रत्यये रूपमिति भाष्यमन्थनकर्तारः ।[119]

अथ कथम्——

ऐक्ष्वाकेषु च मैथिलेषु च फलन्त्वस्माकमद्याशिषः

(अनर्घराघवे ३-५७)

114. See *Prauḍhamanoramā* on *Ata iñ* (4.1.95).
Pradīyatāṃ dāśarathāya maithilī is also quoted in the *Kāśikā* on 4.1.95.
115. To whom is this reference is not clear.
116. I do not find the inclusion of *dākṣi* in the sources available to me.
117. *Nyāsakāra* notes : *prajñādir ayam ākṛtigaṇaḥ.*
118. See the *S.K.* on 1.1.75 (*eṅ prācāṃ deśe*).
119. This is reference to Bhaṭṭoji. See also Notes 35, and 99.
See the *P.M.* on 4.1.157.

इति मुरारिः ।

अत्र इक्ष्वाकुनाम्नो जनपदस्य राजान इति विग्रहे जनपदशब्दात् क्षत्रियादञ् (४-१-१६६) इतिसूत्रेण अञि कृते ञ्यादयस्तद्राजाः (५-३-११९) इत्यनेन तद्राजसंज्ञायाम् तद्राजस्य बहुषु तेनैवास्त्रियाम् (२-४-६२) इति लुकि इक्ष्वाकुषु इति स्यात् इक्ष्वाकूणां दुरापेऽर्थे (रघुवंशे १-७२) इतिवत् । तत् कथम् ऐक्ष्वाकेष्विति प्रयोगः । अत्रोच्यते—नायमञन्तः येनोक्तसंभवः स्यात् । किंतु अयमणन्तः । इक्ष्वाकुशब्दात् कोपधादण् (४-२-१३२) इतिसूत्रेण अणि रूपम् । दाण्डिनायनेत्यादिसूत्रे (६-४-१७४) निपातनात् उकारलोपः । न च अण्प्रत्ययस्य तद्राजस्येति (२-४-६२) लुक् । ञ्यादिमध्ये (५-३-११९ सूत्रं दृश्यताम्) अणो गणनाभावात् तद्राजसंज्ञाया अभावेन तद्राजस्येति लुकः अप्राप्तेः इत्याहुः[120] ।

अथ कथम्—

चत्वारो वयम् ऋत्विजः—

कौरव्याः पशवः——(वेणीसंहारे १-२५)

इति प्रयोगः । अत्र कुरुदेशानां राजान इत्यर्थे कुरुनादिभ्यो ण्यः (४-१-१७२) इतिविहितस्य ण्यप्रत्ययस्य पूर्ववदेव बहुत्वे लुक् स्यादिति चेत्—सत्यम् । कौरव्ये साधवः इति साध्वर्थे तत्र साधुः (४-४-९८) इतिसूत्रेण यत्प्रत्यये रूपसिद्धिः[121] । एतेन तस्यामेव रघोः पाण्ड्याः (रघुवंशे ४-४९) इति पाण्ड्यशब्दोऽप्येवं व्याख्यातः ।

ननु

नैषधे बत वृते दमयन्त्या व्रीडितो न हि बहिर्भवितास्मि (नैषधे ५-७१)

इति श्रीहर्षप्रयोगः कथं संगच्छते । अत्र पूर्ववद् विग्रहे कुरुनादिभ्यः (४-१-१७२) इत्यनेन नादित्वेन ण्यप्रत्ययप्राप्तिरिति चेत्—अत्र वदन्ति । राजन्यर्थे असाधुरेवायम् । तथापि संबन्धसामान्यविवक्षायां तस्येदम् (४-३-१२०) इत्यनेन शैषिकोऽण्[122] व्याख्येय इति ।

120. See *S.K.* and *P.M.* on *Dāṇḍināyana*-etc. (6.4.174).

Murāri uses *aikṣvāka* in many places. See also *A.R.* II.13, and V.5 Rucipati in his commentary on III.57 says thus :

(*ikṣvākuśabdāt*) *tasyāpatyam* (4.1.92) *ityautsargikaḥ aṇ*. (*ikṣvākuśabde*) *dāṇḍināyanetyādinā ukāralopaḥ*.

121. See *Durghaṭavṛtti* and *Ś.K.* on 2.4.62. Bhaṭṭoji says that *raghūṇām* and *yadubhiḥ* are *lākṣaṇikaśabdas*. See also Haradatta 2.4.66 about *raghūṇām*.

122. Bhaṭṭoji quotes the line

sa naiṣadhasyārthapateḥ (XVIII.1)

from the *Raghuvaṃśa*, and gives this answer. See also *S.K.* on 4.1.172. The word *naiṣadha* is used several times by Śrīharṣa. See also for instance *Naiṣadha* III.46; III.79; and XVII.139.

अथ कथम्—

अस्त्रवेदविदयं महीपतिः पार्वतीय इति मावजीगणः ।
(किरातार्जुनीये १३-६७)

इति भारविप्रयोगः ।

तत्र घोरं रघोर्जन्यं पार्वतीयैर्गणैरभूत्[123] । (रघुवंशे ४-७७)

इति कालिदासप्रयोगश्च । अत्र पर्वते भवा इत्यर्थे पर्वताच्च (४-२-१४३) इति छप्रत्यये पर्वतीय इति स्यात् । न तु पार्वतीय इति । तत् कथमत्र दीर्घः इति चेत्—सत्यम् । पर्वतीयस्य इमे इत्यर्थे छान्तादणि रूपमित्याहुः । न च शैषिकात् शैषिको न स्यादिति वाच्यम् । सरूपस्यैव प्रतिषेधात् । असरूपत्वात् छस्य न दोषः ।

अथ कथम्—

औषसातपभयादपलीनं वासरच्छविविरामपटीयः ।
संनिपत्य शनकैरथ निम्नादन्धकारमुदवाप समानि ।। (किरात ६-११)

इति भारविः ।

नूनमुन्नमति यज्वनां पतिः शार्वरस्य तमसो निषिद्धये ।
(कुमार-८-५८)

इति च कालिदासः । अत्र उषसि भवः शर्वर्यां भवः इत्याद्यर्थेषु कालाट्ठञ् (४-३-११) इति सूत्रेण ठञ् प्रत्यये कृते औषसिकः शार्वरिकः इति स्यात् इति चेत्—सत्यम् । समानकालीनं प्राक्कालीनमितिवदपभ्रंशा[124] एवेति पदशास्त्र-निष्णाताः ।

अथ कथम्—

नृपः पुरःस्थैः प्रतिबद्धवर्त्मा पश्चात्तनैः कश्चन नुद्यमानः ।
(यन्त्रस्थसिद्धार्थपदाभिषेकं लब्ध्वाप्यसिद्धार्थममन्यत स्वम् ।।)
(नैषधे-१०-६)

इति श्रीहर्षः ।

लम्बस्तनद्वयमुदस्य निजांसमार्गात्
पृष्ठस्थिरीकृतमहो त्रपया सहैव ।

123. This line from the *Raghu*-IV.77 was quoted by Bhaṭṭoji in his *P.M.* on 4.2.143 (*parvatācca*), and the answer found in our text was in fact given by Bhaṭṭoji there. According to Mallinātha the reading is *parvatīyaiḥ*. There is however a footnote reading of *pārvatīya*, in the *Raghu*.

124. See *S.K.* on *Kālāṭṭhañ* (4.3.11). Mallinātha on *Kirāta*-IX.8 says : *sandhiveletyādinā yogavibhāgād aṇ-pratyayaḥ.*

पश्चात्तनेन शिशुना च शुना च लीढं
नो वेत्ति वेश्यवनिता व्यवहारवेशात् ।। इति च[125] बिल्हणः ।

अत्र पश्चादागत इत्याद्यर्थविग्रहे दक्षिणापश्चात्पुरसस्त्यक् (४-२-९८) इतिसूत्रेण त्यक्प्रत्ययस्य प्राप्तेरीदृशप्रयोगस्य कथं साधुत्वमिति शङ्का । दिग्देश-वाचिनि पश्चाच्छब्दे सावकाशं त्यकं कालवाचकात् ट्युट्युलौ बाधेते परत्वादि-त्यपि न समाधानम् । अग्रादिपश्चाड्डिमच् इतिवार्त्तिकेण (सायंचिरमित्यादि-सूत्रे (४-३-२३) कौमुदी दृश्यताम्) डिमचो विधानात् । तेन ट्युट्युलोर्बाधस्य दुर्वारत्वात् इति चेत्––अत्रोच्यते । प्रमाद एवायमिति केचित् । पश्चात् तन्वन्ति इति तनोतेः पचाद्यच् (३-१-१३४) इति वा कथंचिद् योज्यमित्यन्ये[126] ।

अथ कथम्––

प्रपेदिरे प्राक्तनजन्मविद्याः (कुमार-१-३०)

इति कालिदासः ।

बालं कंचन पञ्चबाणसदृशं चूडापदे लालयन्
पाणौ प्राक्तनसूक्तिसौरभमयीं पात्रीं समारोपयन् ।
वामाङ्के बलवैरिरत्नसुषमावैदग्ध्यमुद्द्योतयन्
स त्यागी चिरमस्तु चेतसि महायोगी वियोगी गुणैः ।।

इति च कथं प्रयोगः । अत्र प्रागित्यव्ययात् द्युप्रागपागुदक्प्रतीचो यत् (४-२-१०१) इति सूत्रेण यत् प्रत्यये प्राच्यमिति स्यात् । कथं प्राक्तनेति पदमिति चेत्–– अत्राहुः[127] कालवाचिनः प्राक्-शब्दात् परत्वात् ट्युट्युलाविति ।

अथ कथम्––

जानक्याः कमलामलाञ्जलिपुटे याः पद्मरागायिताः
न्यस्ता राघवमस्तके च विलसत्कुन्दप्रसूनायिताः ।
स्रस्ताः श्यामलकायकान्तिकलिता या इन्द्रनीलायिताः
मुक्तास्ताः शुभदा भवन्तु भवतां श्रीरामवैवाहिकाः ।।

(महानाटके ?)

125. MSS. D & G read : *bhāṇaḥ* !
MS. B reads : *bāṇaḥ* !
MS. C reads : ..*ṇaḥ* !
MSS. A, E, and F read Bilhaṇaḥ.

126. See *P.M.* on *Dakṣiṇāpaścāt* etc. (4.2.98).

127. See *P.M.* on *Dyuprāgapāg*-etc. (4.2.101).

इति प्रयोगः । अत्र विवाहशब्दात् [128]ठञि प्रत्यये वृद्धौ सत्यां टिड्ढाणञ् (४-१-१५) इत्यादिसूत्रेण ङीपि वैवाहिकी इति स्यात् । बहुवचने च वैवाहिक्य इति भवितव्यम् । तत् कथं वैवाहिकाः इति प्रयोगः इति चेत्--सत्यम् । प्रमाद एवायमिति बहवः । अथ वा विवाहशब्दात् संबन्धार्थे अणि ङीपि वैवाही इति स्त्रियां रूपम् । ततः स्वार्थे कनि (न सामिवचने (५-४-५) इति प्रतिषेधेन ज्ञापिते) केऽणः (७-४-१३) इतिसूत्रेण ईकारस्य ह्रस्वे टाबन्तं रूपं (पुत्रिका कुमारिका इतिवत् वैवाहिका इति) कथंचित् साधनीयमित्येके ।

ननु

निजामयोध्यामपि पावनीमयं
भवन्मयो[129] ध्यायति नावनीपतिः ॥ (नैषधे १२-५)

इति श्रीहर्षप्रयोगः कथम् । अत्र भवत्या विकार इति विग्रहे मयट् प्रत्यये (मयट् वा एतयोरित्यादिसूत्रेण---४-१-१४३) कथं [130]पुंवद्भावः । तस्य ठक्-छसोश्चेति वार्त्तिकरीत्या भावत्काः भवदीयाः इत्यत्रैव संभवात् । [131]अन्यत्र

128. MSS. read : *kani* here. This should be due to mistake of some scribe or other. Later the word *kani* in this context occurs in the text. But in *vaivāhika* the suffix should be *ṭhañ*. So I surmised *ṭhañi*. Mallinātha in his commentary on the *Kumāra*-VII.2, explaining *vaivāhika* says : *vivāhaḥ prayojanam eṣām iti vaivāhikāni. Prayojanam* (5.1.109) iti *ṭhañ*. On *prayojana* of the rule 5.1.109, Bhaṭṭoji says : *prayojanam = phalam, kāraṇaṃ ca.*

129. See also *Naiṣadha* III.113 (*bhavadviyoga*), IV.121 (*bhavadvidhā*) VIII.73 (*bhavadakṣivāsī*). See also the *Kādambarī* :

atimahat khalu bhavaddarśanāt prabhṛti me kutūhalam asmin
(p. 291; N.S.P. 1948).

130. There seems to have been some difficulty in having a correct interpretation of the rule regarding the *puṃvadbhāva* (i.e. retaining the masculine stem, though the person referred to may be a female in a given context, as is clear from the *vigrahavākya*). Some earlier writers quoted the following rule :

sarvanāmnaḥ samāse pūrvaṃ puṃvat,

and noted it to be a *vārttika*. But there is no *vārttika* like this traceable. It was to the credit of Bhaṭṭoji, it seems, who pointed out the inexistence of such a *vārttika*, and made clear that it was an *Iṣṭi* of Patañjali in the form of *sarvanāmno vṛttimātre puṃvadbhāvaḥ*.

See his *S.K.* under *Ṭhakchasoś ca* (on 6.3.35,—*Tasilādiṣu* etc.) and the *P.M.* in this context. The *Iṣṭi* : *sarvanāmno vṛttimātre puṃvadbhāvaḥ* is found in the *Mahābhāṣya* under 2.2.26, and under 5.3.28. See also Note 132.

131. The *pūrvapakṣa* raised here is owing to the ignorance of the *Iṣṭi*, and consequently is based on the view that *puṃvadbhāva* is not possible in all the cases, but possible only in *bhāvatka* and *bhavadīya* (the cases of *ṭhak* and *chas* suffixes). See the *Veṇīsaṃhāra* V.9 (*bhavatīsutakṣayakaraḥ*), and the *Śākuntala* : after V.24 (*atrabhavatīpratyayāt*). See also Jagaddhara on *Veṇīsaṃhāra* V.9.

तदप्राप्तेरिति चेत्——सत्यम् । सर्वनाम्नो वृत्तिमात्रे पुंवद्भाव इति [132]भाष्यकारेष्ट्या (दिङ्नामान्यन्तराले-२-२-२६——इति सूत्रे-दक्षिणोत्तराभ्यामतसुच्——५-३-२८- इतिसूत्रे च भाष्यं दृश्यताम्) वृत्तिमात्रे इति मात्रशब्देन कात्स्न्यार्थकेन अन्यत्रापि वृत्तौ——समासे तद्धितान्तरे च——पुंवद्भावः साधुरेवेति वदन्ति ।

अथ कथम्——

पाशं दधानः करबद्धवासं विभुर्बभावाप्यम् अवाप्य देहम् ॥

(नैषधे-१४-६७)

इति श्रीहर्षः । अत्र अपां विकार इत्यर्थे एकाचो नित्यम् (नित्यं वृद्धशरादिभ्यः -४-३-१४४ इति सूत्रे कौमुदी दृश्यताम्) इत्यनेन मयट्प्राप्तेः अम्मयम् इति स्यात् । तत् कथम् आप्यमिति चेत्——अत्र वदन्ति अपां संबन्धीत्यर्थे तस्येदम् (४-३-१२०) इत्यण्प्रत्यये ततः स्वार्थे ष्यणि रूपमिति[133] ।

अथ कथम्——

ये यन्मयाः स्मृता——तेषामेतास्तु तन्मयाः ।
विना प्रमेहमप्येता जायन्ते हृष्टमेधसः ॥ इति मधुकोशः ।
अयं विषाङ्को विधुरेष नूनं कलाः समस्ता अपि तन्मयास्ताः ।
योगौषधे येन समं न यान्ति केचिद् वियोगादरुचिं भजन्ते ॥ (?)

इति च । अत्र एतास्तन्मयाः इत्यादौ मयटष्टित्वात् टिड्ढाणञ् (४-१-१५) इत्यादिना ङीप् स्यात् इति चेत्[134]अत्राहुः ——क्वचिदपवादविषयेप्युत्सर्गोऽभिनिविशते इति परिभाषया टाप् भवतीति कथंचिद् व्याख्येयमित्याहुः ।

अथ कथम्——

काव्यं यशसेऽर्थकृते व्यवहारविदे शिवेतरक्षतये (काव्यप्रकाशे) इति मम्मटः । अत्र कवेर्भावः कर्म वेति विग्रहे इगन्ताच्च लघुपूर्वात् (५-१-१३१) इति सूत्रेण अण् प्रत्ययः स्यात् । ततश्च कावम् इति रूपं भवेत् इति चेत्——अत्र वदन्ति गुणवचनब्राह्मणादिभ्यः (५-१-१२४) इत्यनेन ष्यञि [135]भविष्यतीति । केचित् तु कु शब्दे इति धातोः ओरावश्यके (३-१-१२५) इतिसूत्रेण ण्यत् प्रत्यये रूपमित्याहुः[136] ।

132. The answer is supplied by the *Iṣṭi*, which records the *puṃvadbhāva* in all the *vṛttis* (i.e. *samāsa*, and all *Taddhita* cases, not only *ṭhak* and *chas*). See Note 130.

133. See *S.K.* on 4.3.144 (*nityaṃ vṛddha*-etc.). Bhaṭṭoji gives this answer. See also the *Durghaṭavṛtti* on 4.3.144.

134. See the *Paribhāṣenduśekhara*.

135. The *Kāśikā* says : *brāhmaṇādiṣu kaviśabdo draṣṭavyaḥ* (on 5.1.131). See also *S.K.* and *P.M.* on 5.1.131.

136. Bhaṭṭoji says in his *P.M.* : *yadyapi kudhātoḥ Orāvaśyake* (3.1.125) *iti ṇyati kāvyam iti susādham, tathāpi kaveḥ karmetyarthe kāvam iti syad iti praśnaḥ.*

अथ कथम्—

वृद्ध्याजीवश्च वार्धुषिः इत्यमरः ।
न स्तेनः स्यान्न वार्धुषिः । वार्धुष्यं लवणक्रिया ।

वार्धुषिः सप्तकं यथा इत्यादि च । अत्र वृद्ध्यर्थं प्रयच्छतीति विग्रहे प्रयच्छति गर्ह्यम् (४-४-३०) इति सूत्रेण गर्ह्यार्थे ठकि कृते वृद्धेर्वृधुषिभावो वक्तव्यः इति वार्त्तिकेन वृधुषिभावे वार्धुषिक इति स्यात् । कथं वार्धुषिरिति चेत्—सत्यम् । स्वच्छन्दवाचः कवय इति [137]हरदत्तः समादधौ ।

अथ कथम्—

तदनु कदनभूमेः खेचरैः स्तूयमानः
प्रसभमवनिभर्तुः सोदरो निर्जगाम । (राघवपाण्डवीये १०–४२)

इति कविराजः ।

अपन्थानं तु गच्छन्तं सोदरोऽपि विमुञ्चति (अनर्घ-१–४) इति मुरारिश्च । अत्र सोदराद् यः (४-४-१०६) इतिसूत्रेण यप्रत्यये सोदर्य इति स्यादिति चेत्—अत्राहुः[138] । सह-समानम् उदरं यस्येति बहुव्रीहौ समानार्थकसहशब्दस्य वोपसर्जनस्य (६-३-८२) इतिसूत्रेण सभावे रूपमिदम् । न चात्रापि यप्रत्ययः कुतो नेति वाच्यम् । समानोदरे शयितः (४-४-१०८) इति पूर्वसूत्रार्थविषयत्वात् यप्रत्ययस्येति नात्र यप्रत्ययः । एतेन यत्र भ्राता सहोदरः (वाल्मीकिरामायणे युद्धकाण्डे १०१ सर्गे १५ श्लोकः) इत्यपि व्याख्यातम् ।

अथ कथम्—

ततो यथावद् विहिताध्वराय (रघुवंशे ५-१९) इति कालिदासः ।

अत्र यथावदित्यत्र तदर्हम् (५-१-११७) इतिसूत्रेण वतिप्रत्ययो वक्तव्यः । स च द्वितीयान्तादेव अर्हतीत्यर्थे संभवति । यथाशब्दस्य अव्ययत्वात् द्वितीयान्तत्वं कथम्—इति चेत्—अत्र वदन्ति ।[139] यथाशब्दो वृत्तिविषये सत्त्वार्थकः । तथात्वं यथात्वम् इत्यादिषु त्वतलादिदर्शनात् । तथा च द्वितीयान्तार्थकाद् यथाशब्दादर्हार्थे वतिः । यथा-योग्यताम् अर्हति विधानम् आख्यानं वेत्यर्थाद् वतिः साधुरेवेति कृत्वा यथावदिति युक्तम् इति ।

137. Printed editions of the *Padamañjarī* read : *svacchandavācaḥ ṛṣayaḥ*. Bhaṭṭoji's *P.M.* (on 4.4.30) quotes Haradatta's line as *svacchandavācaḥ kavayaḥ*.

138. See *P.M.* on 4.4.109. See also *S.K.* on 6.3.84.

139. See *P. M.* and the *Tattvabodhinī* on 5.1.117.

अथ कथम्——

अवतीर्य यदोर्वंशे भगवान् सात्वतां पतिः (भागवते?) इति प्रयोगः । अत्र सत्त्वम् एषामस्तीति विग्रहे तदस्यास्त्यस्मिन्निति (५-२-९४) मतुपि मादुपधायाः (८-२-९) इत्यनेन वत्वे च सत्त्ववताम् इति स्यात् । तत् कथं सात्वताम् इति चेत्——सत्यम् । सत्त्वमेषामस्तीत्यर्थे एव सस्य दीर्घो वस्य लोपश्च छान्दसत्वादिति श्रीधरस्वामिनः । वस्तुतस्तु अनुपसर्गाल्लिम्पेत्यादिसूत्रे (३-१-१३८) सातिः सौत्रो धातुरिति काशिका । सुखार्थ इति च रक्षितः । सातिर्हेतुमण्ण्यन्त इति हरदत्तः । तस्मात् क्विपि सात् इति रूपम् । सातयति सुखयतीत्यर्थे सात् परमात्मा । (एष ह्येवानन्दयतीति श्रुतेः तस्य सुखयितृत्वावगमात्——इति बालमनोरमा।) स एषामिति सात्वन्तो भक्ताः इति [140]भाष्यज्ञाः ।

अय कथम्——

पश्यामि तामित इतः पुरतश्च पश्चात्

(मालतीमाधवे १-४३)

इति भवभूतिः ।

लोभस्य पुरतः केऽमी सत्यास्तेयाप्रतिग्रहाः

(प्रबोधचन्द्रोदये १-१५)

इति कृष्णमिश्रश्च । इयं च तेऽन्या पुरतो विडम्बना

(कुमार ५-७०)

इति कालिदासश्च । पुरत इति रूपम् अतसुच् प्रत्ययेन साधनीयम् । तन्न घटते । तथा हि——पूर्वाधरावराणामसिपुरधवश्चैषाम् (५-३-३९) इति सूत्रेण असिप्रत्यये उत्तरसूत्रेण अस्तातौ च पूर्वादीनां पुरादयः आदेशा विहिताः । तेन पुरः पुरस्तात् इति रूपेण भवितव्यम् । पूर्वशब्दाद् अतसुच्प्रत्ययविधायकसूत्राभावात्

140. This is a reference to Bhaṭṭoji. His *Ś.K.* has a good discussion about this on 3.1.138. Bhaṭṭoji takes *sāt* with *bhāve kvip* in the sense of *brahman.* The *Bālamanoramā* explains it with *kartari kvip* also. Bhaṭṭoji quotes in his Ś.K. (3.1.138) the line *sātvatāṃ patiḥ* from the *Viṣṇusahasranāma-*.

In the context of *sātvatī vṛtti* and *sātvato guṇaḥ* (pp. 86, & 96; N.Ś.; Vol. III. GOS), Abhinava says thus:

sat = sattvam = prakāśaḥ. tat vidyate yatra tat sat + van = manaḥ.taṣmin (satvati manasi) bhavaḥ sātvato guṇaḥ (p. 96, *Ibid.*)

(....Similarly on *sātvatī (vṛtti)* he says:

sat = satvarūpaṃ vidyate yeṣāṃ te satvantaḥ. teṣām iyaṃ sātvatī (p. 86, *Ibid.*)

In these places the printed edition has corrupt readings. What is given here is the reading as corrected by me.

अतसुचि पूर्वशब्दस्य पुरादेशविधायकसूत्राभावाच्च पुरत इति रूपं [141]चिन्त्यम् इति भाषावृत्तिः। कश्चित्तु विभाषा परावराभ्याम् (५-३-२९) इतिसूत्रे विभाषेति-योगविभागात् पूर्वशब्दाद् अतसुच्। अस्ताति च (५-३-४०) इति चकारस्य अनुक्तसमुच्चयार्थत्वात् पूर्वशब्दस्यातसुचि पुरादेशश्च। तेन पुरत इति रूपमिति समाहितवान्। तन्निर्मूलमिति समानाकालीनं प्राक्कालीनमित्यादिवत् प्रामादिकमेवेति [142]बहवः। यद्वा—पुर अग्रगमने इति धातोः चौरादिकात् णिजभावे उगुपधज्ञाप्रीकिरः कः (३-१-१३५) इतिसूत्रेण कप्रत्यये पुरमिति रूपम्। ततस्सार्वविभक्तिकस्तसिः। तेन पुरत इति [143]साधनीयम्।

अथ कथम्—

अव्रतानाममन्त्राणां जातिमात्रोपजीविनाम्।
सहस्रशः समेतानां परिषत्त्वं न विद्यते ॥ ( )

इति प्रयोगः। अत्र संख्यैकवचनाच्च वीप्सायाम् (५-४-४३) इतिसूत्रेण शस् वक्तव्यः। स दुर्लभः। नह्यत्र वीप्सा नापि कारकत्वमस्तीति चेत्—अत्र [144]वदन्ति। सहस्रं सहस्रं ये समेतास्तेषामपि परिषत्त्वं नेत्यर्थः। तथा च समवायक्रियां प्रति कर्तृत्वं वीप्सा चास्त्येवेति।

अथ कथम्—

मायाप्रपञ्चजगदर्णवभीतभीतः (चौरपञ्चाशति—१३)

(श्रौत्तराहपाठानुसारेण)

इति बिल्हणः।

मन्दमन्दमुदितः प्रययौ खं भीतभीत इव शीतमयूखः ॥

(किरात-९-२६)

इति भारविश्च। अत्र प्रकारे गुणवचनस्य (८-१-१२) इतिसूत्रेण सादृश्ये द्योत्ये द्वित्वं कर्मधारयवद्भावश्चेति वक्तव्यम्। इवशब्देनैव सादृश्यस्योक्ततया इह प्रकारे द्वित्वायोगात् कथमयं प्रयोगः इति चेत्—सत्यम्। भीतेभ्योऽपि भीतः इति कथंचिद् व्याख्येयम्। तेनातिभीत इति फलितोऽर्थ [145]इत्याहुः।

141. See *Durghaṭavṛtti* on 5.3.40, which quotes the *Bhāṣāvṛtti* also. See also *P.M.* on this.

142. See *P.M.* on 5.3.39 (*pūrvādharāvara*-etc.).

143. See Nāgeśa's *Marmaprakāśa* on the *Rasagaṅgādhara* (p.172; N.S.P., 1894). It is not clear whether our author is quoting the view of Nāgeśa. See the Introduction.

144. See *P.M.* on 5.3.43 (*Saṅkhyaikavacanācca* etc.).

145. See *Durghaṭavṛtti*, *P.M.*, and *T.B.* on 8.1.12 (*Prakāre*).

ननु कथम्

सख्या चित्रितमम्बुजं स्तनतटे नो मर्दितं स्वेच्छया
मन्दं मन्दमलग्नदन्तमधुरं चिक्रीड बालासमम् ।

इति [146]काव्यकण्ठाभरणे । अत्र वीप्सार्थस्यासंभवात् नित्यवीप्सयोः (८-१-४) इत्यस्याप्राप्त्या प्रकारे गुणवचनस्येति सूत्रेणैव द्वित्वं वक्तव्यम् । तदा च कर्मधारयवद्भावात् सुपो लुक् स्यात् इति चेत्—अत्राहुः कथंचिद् वीप्सायामेव [147]द्विर्भावो निर्वाह्य इति । क्रीडनक्रियावस्थासु भेदं परिकल्प्य कथंचिद् वीप्सा बोध्या [148]इति । प्रकारार्थे तु सुसाधः कवीनां प्रयोगः । मन्दमन्दमुदितः प्रययौ खम् (किरात-९-२६)

—मन्दमन्दमितरेतरमूचुः (नैषधे ५-६६)
इत्यादिवदिति ज्ञेयमिति दिक् ।

इति श्रीसाहित्यकण्टकोद्धारे पूर्वपरिच्छेदे
सुबन्तप्रक्रिया समाप्ता ।

146. I am unable to trace this work or the verse.

147. See Vāmana's *K.A.S.* V.2.85, and the *Vṛtti* thereon. Mallinātha on *Meghasandeśa* I.9 says:

atra vīpsāyām eva kathaṃcid dviruktir nirvāhyā.

148. See *P.M.* on 8.1.12, which quotes *khinnaḥ khinnaḥ* etc. and notes thus: *ekasyāpy avasthāsu bhedaṃ parikalpya kathaṃcid vīpsā boddhyā.*

अथ उत्तरपरिच्छेदः

(साहित्यकण्टकोद्धारे)

तिङ्प्रत्ययानुसारेण[149] दूषणं भूषणं मया ।
साहित्यकण्टकोद्धारे लिख्यते विदुषां मुदे ॥

कदा भविष्यते वासः कटकेषु महीभृताम् ॥ (दोषप्रकरणे २१५ पुटे) इति च्युतसंस्कारोदाहरणं प्रतापरुद्रीये । ईदृशप्रयोगो दुष्टत्वाद् वर्जनीय इति प्रदर्शनार्थमिदम् । आधृषीयप्राप्त्यर्थकस्यैव भूधातोरात्मनेपदित्वम् । न तु सत्तार्थकस्य भौवादिकस्येति दोषः—इति केचित्[150] । अन्ये तु[151] आधृषीयप्राप्त्यर्थकभूधातोः णिजन्तादेवात्मनेपदम् । न तु केवलात् (अण्यन्तात्) इति अण्यन्तस्यात्मनेपदप्रयोगः (आधृषीयस्यापि) दुष्ट इति वदन्ति । अत एव प्रतापरुद्रीयकारेण मूले एव स्फुटीकृतमित्थम्—भविष्यते इति भवतेरात्मनेपदित्वं शब्दशास्त्रविरुद्धमिति[152] ।

अथ कथम्—

निश्चोतन्ते सुतनु कबरीबिन्दवो यावदेते
यावन्मध्यः स्तनमुकुलयोरार्द्रभावं जहाति ।
यावत्सान्द्रप्रतनुपुलकोद्भेदवत्यङ्गयष्टि-
स्तावद् गाढं वितर सकृदप्यङ्कपालीं प्रसीद ॥ इति ।

(मालतीमाधवे ८-२)

149. MSS. A, C, and F have the section on the *Kṛdanta-prayoga* here, and have subsequently the portion on *Tiṅanta*.

MSS. B, D, E, and G, have the portion on the *Tiṅanta* first here, and then that on the *Kṛdanta*. This seems to be the correct order intended by the author, who seems to follow the order of the *Siddhāntakaumudī*. The MSS. A, C, and F also, after completing the portion on the *Tiṅanta* have again some part of the *Kṛdanta*. So I decided to give the portion on the *Tiṅanta* first, and then that on the *Kṛdanta*.

See also Note 239.

150. Kumārasvāmin while commenting on this (p. 216) says:
prāptyarthasyaiva bhavater ātmanepaditvam;
na tu sattārthasyeti vaiyākaraṇāh.

151. Bhaṭṭoji in his *S.K.* on this root in *Curādi* says:
ṇic-sanniyoganaivātmanepadam ityeke.

152. See *Pratāparudrīya* (Balamano. edn; 1950; p. 216)

अत्र श्चुतिर्[153] क्षरणे इति धातोः परस्मैपदित्वात् कथमात्मनेपदप्रयोगः इति चेत्—सत्यम् । ईदृशः प्रमाद एवेति शास्त्रशरणाः ।

अथ कथम्—

वैदेशिकः स्वकुललाञ्छनतां विधत्ते
तद् भूपतिः [153a]क्षमति किं श्रुतमेव नास्ति । (चौरपञ्चाशत्-६१)
(श्रौत्तराहपाठः)

इति चौरपञ्चाशति । अत्र क्षमूष् सहने इति धातोः अनुदात्तेत्त्वात् कथं परस्मैपदप्रयोगः । आत्मनेपदेन हि भवितव्यम् इति चेत्—प्रमाद एवायमित्याहुः । अनुदात्तेत्त्वलक्षणमात्मनेपदमनित्यमिति[154] वा समाधेयम् ।

अथ कथम्—

उदयति स्म तदद्भुतमालिभिर्धरणिभृद् भुवि तत्र विमृश्य यत् ।
(नैषधे ४-१८)

इति श्रीहर्षः । उदयति विततोर्ध्वरश्मिरज्जौ (माघ काव्ये ४-२०) इति माघश्च । अत्र अय गताविति धातोरनुदात्तेत्त्वेनात्मनेपदित्वात् ।

मोहः कोऽयमहो महानुदयते लोकस्य शोकावहः (प्रबोधचन्द्रोदये (५-१४) इतिवदात्मनेपदस्यैव युक्तत्वात् इति चेत्—सत्यम् ।

इट किट कटी गतौ इत्यत्र प्रश्लिष्टस्य इधातोः रूपमिदम् । तस्य परस्मैपदित्वादिति [155]समादधुः ।

153. There are two roots recorded in the *Dhātupāṭha* in *Bhvādi*. One is *Cyutir āsecane* (without *ś* in the beginning) and the other *ścutir kṣaraṇe*. The second one has palatal *ś* in the beginning, and of this there are two readings handed down. According to one reading, there is *y* as a third consonant (after *c*), and according to the other there is no *y* (as *ścutir*). Bhaṭṭoji (in *S.K.*) notes: *yakārarahito'py ayam*. In *P.M.* he quotes:

tathā ca prayujyate madhuścutam ghṛtam iva supūtam iti.

In any case the root is only *parasmaipadin*. Hence the doubt.

153-a. The printed edn. however has the reading as:

śrutvāpi tat khalu bhavān kṣamate'tra citram.

Our author perhaps had access to the different reading.

154. See *K.A.S.V.*2.3, and the *Vṛtti* thereon. Also see *S.K.* on the root *cakṣiṅ vyaktāyāṃ vāci*, where Bhaṭṭoji also notes the same point.

155. See *S. K.* after *Upasargasyāyatau* (8.2.19), where this answer is noted by Bhaṭṭoji. He also notes:

yadvā anudāttettvalakṣaṇamātmanepadam anityam iti.

अथ कथम्—

श्रीबिल्हणं निजगुरुं प्रणिपत्य साक्षात्
तं [156]हर्षयां नृपतिम् आस सरस्वतीं च ।

(चौरपञ्चाशति श्रौत्तराहपाठः २१)

इति बिल्हणः । अत्र कृञ्चानुप्रयुज्यते लिटि (३-१-४०) इतिसूत्रेण कृभ्वस्तीनाम् अनुप्रयोगेणाव्यवहितेन भवितव्यम् । कथमेवं व्यवहितप्रयोग इति चेत् —सत्यम् । प्रामादिका एवेदृशा इति शब्दशास्त्रधुरीणाः [157]। नच विपरीतप्रयोगनिवृत्तिमात्रे सूत्रस्य [158]तात्पर्यमस्त्विवति वाच्यम् । विपर्यासनिवृत्त्यर्थं व्यवहितनिवृत्त्यर्थं च (३-१-४२ इतिसूत्रे) इति वार्त्तिकविरोधापत्तेः । अत एव शब्दशास्त्रज्ञाः कवयः आमन्तादव्यवहितोत्तरमेव कृभ्वस्तीनां प्रयोगमाद्रियन्ते । तथा च माघः

तस्यातपत्रं बिभरां बभूवे (३-२) इति ।

तपर्तुपूर्तावपि मेदसां भरा विभावरीभि बिभरां बभूविरे (नैषधे १-४१)

इति श्रीहर्षश्च ।

अथ कथम्—

अनुक्तमप्यूहति पण्डितो जनः
परेङ्गितज्ञानफला हि बुद्धयः ।। (पञ्चतन्त्रे १-४४ दृश्यताम्)

156. This is quoted to illustrate the split periphrastic perfect (i.e. *harṣayām nṛpatim āsa*, instead of the regular *harṣayām āsa*).

MSS. A, C, & F read : *harṣayām* etc.

MSS. B, D, & G read: *dūṣayām* etc.

MS. E is not clear.

157. See *Padamañjarī* and *Ś.K.* On 3.1.40. Both writers consider these usages to be incorrect in Classical Sanskrit. The author of the *Mukhabhūṣaṇa* says on page 54 thus:

> *tasmād bhāṣāyām api vyavahitaścāvyavahitaś ca anuprayogo bhavatīti sthitam. Padamañjarīkārasyāpi ayam eva rāddhāntah.*

The statement about *Padamañjarīkāra* does not seem to be correct, as Haradatta says the other way. See *op. cit.*

Mallinātha however does not agree with Haradatta completely. According to Mallinātha if the intervening expression is an *upasarga* in the examples such as *ukṣāṃ pra cakruḥ* (Bhaṭṭi III.5), and *bibhayāṃ pra cakārāsau* (Bhaṭṭi VI.2), the usage is correct. Only if it happens to be other than an *upasarga* in examples such as *taṃ pātayāṃ prathamam āsa* (*Raghu.* IX.61), and *prabhraṃśayāṃ yo nahuṣaṃ cakāra* (*Raghu* XIII.36), and *saṃyojayāṃ vidhivad āsa* (Ibid. XVI.86)—*prathamam* etc.—, Mallinātha considers such split usages to be incorrect ones. See his commentary on Bhaṭṭi III.5, where he has a very good discussion.

158. See *T.B.* on 3;1.40.

अत्र ऊहतेरनुदात्तेत्त्वात् अनुदात्तङित आत्मनेपदम् (१-३-१२) इतिसूत्रेण आत्मनेपदप्राप्तिः (ऊहते इति स्यात्) इति चेत्—सत्यम्। चक्षिङ धातोः (इकारे सत्यप्यनुदात्ते इत्संज्ञके) ङित्-करणसामर्थ्यात् अनुदात्तेत्त्वलक्षणमात्मनेपदमनित्यमिति ज्ञापनात् नात्रात्मनेपदमिति [159]समाधेयमित्याहुः। केचित्तु भ्रोहति इत्याङ्पूर्वं पठित्वा (अर्थात् आ इत्युपसर्गपूर्वकस्य ऊहति इत्यस्य प्रयोगमाश्रित्य) उपसर्गादस्यत्यूह्योः (वेत्तेर्विभाषा इत्यत्र कौमुदी दृश्यताम्) इति वार्त्तिकेन परस्मैपदित्वमिति (समूहति इतिवत्) साधुत्वं व्याख्येयमिति समादधुः। एतेन[160] (अनुदात्तेत्त्वलक्षणमात्मनेपदमनित्यमिति स्वीकारेण)

स एवायं नागः सहति[161] कलभेभ्यः परिभवम्

इति प्रयोगोऽपि (सहति इति परस्मैपदे) [161]व्याख्यातो भवति।

अथ कथम्—

कूले[162] यदूदिथ वचस्तपनात्मजायाः

इति[163] (पल्लवः)[164]। अत्र ऊदिथेति वदतेः लिटि मध्यमपुरुषस्यैकवचने रूपमिति वक्तव्यम्। तत्तु न घटते। तथा हि—वदतेः सिपादेशभूते थलि परे लिट्यभ्यासस्योभयेषाम् (६-१-१७) इति सूत्रेण अभ्यासवकारस्य संप्रसारणे

159. See *P.M.* on the root *ūha vitarke.*
See also the *Durghaṭavṛtti* on 3.1.12.

160. Bhaṭṭoji quotes this line in his *S.K.* under the root *ṣaha marṣaṇe* in *Curādi* (1810). Bhūṣaṇabhaṭṭa uses *duḥkhāny api sahanti* (K.p.532).

161. The portion from *etena* to *vyākhyāto bhavati* is missing in MS. G.
MSS. A, B, C, D, E & F read: *iti murārir vyākhyātaḥ.* I do not find this line in the *A.R.*, or in Rucipati's commentary. Under 1.3.12 the *Durghaṭavṛtti* quotes: *sa sahet na kathaṃ tuṣāram* (p.15).

162. MS. E seems to read: *jāte.* Several syllables in the line are not clear in this MS.
MSS. A, B, C, D, & F read: *kūle.*
In MS. G some lines including this quotation are missing.

163. MS. A reads: *tūppilyallaḥ.*
MS. B does not have any name of the author.
MS. C reads: *tūppillaḥ* (or *tūvūri pillaḥ* ?)
MS. D reads: *tūparavellaḥ* !!!
MS. E reads: *mātrārivillācāryaḥ* !!!
It may take several months to get our brains back to normal, which may go off the track while reading the writings of these scribes!!!

164. Bhaṭṭoji quotes this line in his *P.M.*, (p.413; C.S.S., 1928) and attributes it to one Pallava. It is not clear whether this has some thing to do with *Pallava* or *Kalpapallava* attributed to *Ambāprasāda-saciva* (See Introduction to *Kalpalatāviveka*, p.2; L. D. Series 17, 1968, Ahmedabad).

उवदियेति रूपं स्यात् । प्रकृतिभूतवकारस्य संप्रसारणविधायकसूत्राभावात् । न च वचिस्वपियजादीनां किति (६-१-१५) सूत्रेण धातुगतवकारस्यैव संप्रसारणं भवत्विति वाच्यम् । तस्य किति [165]प्रत्यये परे एव प्रवृत्तेः । तस्माद् ऊदियेति रूपं प्रामादिकमेवेत्याहुः ।

अथ कथम्—

त्यजस्व कोपं कुलकीर्तिनाशनं भजस्व धर्मं कुलकीर्तिवर्धनम् ।
प्रसीद जीवेम सबान्धवा वयं प्रदीयतां दाशरथाय मैथिली ॥

(हनुमन्नाटके ७-१०)

इति प्रयोगः । अत्र त्यज हानाविति धातोः परस्मैपदित्वात् इति चेत्—सत्यम् । प्रामादिक एवायमिति प्रामाणिकाः ।

अथ कथम्—

कदा नु होष्ये[166] कुशिकात्मजाय (उदारराघवे) इति शाकल्यमल्लः ।

अत्र हु दानादनयोरितिधातोः परस्मैपदित्वात् कथमात्मनेपदप्रयोगः इति चेत्—निरर्गलाः कवय इति [167]समादधुः ।

अथ कथम्—

त्वयि मत्सरादिव निरस्तदयः सुतरां क्षिणोति खलु तां मदनः

(६-६३)

इति माघः । अत्र क्षिणोतीति रूपं क्षि हिंसायामिति धातोरिति वक्तव्यम् । तत्र छन्दसीति गणसूत्रात् छन्दस्येवायं प्रयोगो युक्तः न तु लोके इति चेत्—प्रमाद एवेति केचित् । [168]भाषायामपीत्यन्ये ।

165. See the rule *Asaṃyogāt* etc. (1.2.5), which specifies that only those suffixes which do not have "*p*" as an indicatory letter (i.e. *apit*) are counted as *kit* technically. Second person singular basic suffix (*sip*) has "*p*". So it cannot be counted as *kit*.

166. MSS. A, C, E, & F read the usage of *jayāya senānyam* here, and then the usage *kadā nu hoṣye*.

MSS. B, D, & G read the example: *kadā nu hoṣye* first, and then the other: *ayāya senānyam*.

167. See *P.M.* in the beginning of the *Juhotyādi*. Bhaṭṭoji says:
hoṣye ityādikas tu keṣāṃcit prayogaḥ prāmādika eva.

Bhaṭṭoji does not mention here the name of the *Udārarāghava* or Śākalyamalla, whom Bhaṭṭoji knows. He mentions in his *Ś.K.* (on 3.1.29; p. 363; CSS. 1929) Bhaṭṭamalla (who is same as Śākalyamalla) and his *Ākhyātacandrikā*. The present usage also might have been quoted by Bhaṭṭoji from the *Udārarāghava*.

168. See *S.K.* on the root *Kṣi hiṃsāyām* (*svādi*). Bhaṭṭoji quotes the line:
na tad yaśaś śastrabhṛtāṃ kṣiṇoti (*Raghu.*II.40).

This answer is also noted by him.

अथ कथम्—

जयाय सेनान्यमुशन्ति देवाः (कुमार–३-१५)

इति प्रयोगः । वशधातोरपि छन्दोविषयत्वात् इति चेत्—भाषायामपि प्रयोगो दृश्यते एवेति वदन्ति—वष्टि भागुरिरल्लोपम् इति यथा ।

अथ कथम्—

आदावञ्जनपुञ्जलिप्तवपुषां श्वासानिलोल्लासित-
प्रोत्सर्पद्विरहानलेन च ततः संतापितानां दृशाम् ।
संप्रत्येव निषेकमश्रुपयसा देवस्य चेतोभुवो
भल्लीनामिव पानकर्म कुरुते कामं कुरङ्गेक्षणा ।। (काव्यप्रकाशे-७ उल्लासे)

इत्यत्र कुरुते इति प्रयोगः । यजन्ति याजकाः इतिवत् प्रधानक्रियाफलस्य कर्त्रा असंबन्धे कर्त्रभिप्रायक्रियाफलस्याभावात् स्वरितञ्जितः कर्त्रभिप्राये क्रियाफले (१३-७२) इति विहितमात्मनेपदं कथं युज्यताम्—इति चेत्—प्रमाद एवायमिति काव्यप्रकाशकारादयः ।

अथ कथम्—

अर्थानां प्रविवेचनाय जगतामन्तस्तमश्शान्तये
सन्मार्गस्य विलोकनाय गतये लोकस्य यात्रार्थिनः ।
तत्तत्तामसभूतभीतय इमां विद्यावतां प्रीतये
व्यातेने[169] किरणावलीमुदयनः सत्तर्कतेजोमयीम् ।।

इत्युदयनाचार्याः (किरणावल्यम्) ।

सरस्वतीदत्तवरप्रसादश्चक्रे सुबन्धुः सुजनैकबन्धुः

इति (वासवदत्तायाम् (आदौ) सुबन्धुश्च । अत्र व्यातेने चक्रे इत्यादौ जीवति कर्तरि पारोक्ष्यासंभवात् कथं परोक्षे लिट् (३-२-११५) इति सूत्रेण लिट्—इति चेत्—सत्यम् । णलुत्तमो वा (७-१-९१) इति सूत्रात् ज्ञापकात् कर्त्रपरोक्षत्वेऽपि लिटः साधुत्वम् । यद्यत्रासाधुत्वं तदा उत्तमपुरुषः कर्त्रपरोक्षः एवेति कृत्वा परोक्षे विधीयमानस्य लिटः उत्तमे प्राप्तिरेव नास्ति । ततश्च कथमाह णलो विकल्पं सूत्रकारः । तस्मात् कर्त्रपरोक्षत्वेऽपि लिटः साधुत्वं ज्ञाप्यते इति केचन समादधुः । अन्ये तु आशंसायां भूतवच्च (३-३-१३२) इत्यनेनाशंसायां लिडित्याहुः । परे तु क्रियानुकूलशक्तिमतां व्यापाराविष्टानां साधनानां पारोक्ष्यमिह विवक्षितम् । तेन क्रियानाविष्टसाधनमात्रप्रत्यक्षेऽपि लिट् भवत्येव । अयं पपाच । त्वं पेचिथ इतिवत् [170]वदन्ति ।

169. See Kauṇḍabhaṭṭa's *Bhūṣaṇasāra*; the *lakārārthanirṇaya* (on *liṭ*). Kauṇḍabhaṭṭa quotes this line of Udayana and considers it to be incorrect.
170. See *P.M.* on *Parokṣe liṭ* (3.2.115).

अथ कथम्—

तुलयति स्म विलोचनतारकाः कुरवकस्तबकव्यतिषङ्गिनि (६-४)

इति माघः । अत्र तुल उन्माने इति चौरादिकस्य णिचि पुगन्तेतिसूत्रेण (७-३-८६) गुणे तोलयति इति स्यात् यद्गुञ्जासमतोलनम् इत्यादिवत्—इति चेत् अत्र वदन्ति । तुल्यार्थैरतुलोपमाभ्याम् (२-३-७२) इतिसूत्रादेव निपातनात् तुलाशब्दः साधुः । ततः तत् करोति तदाचष्टे (गणसूत्रं चुरादौ दृश्यताम्) इत्यनेन णिचि सति इदं रूपं [171]सिद्धयति इति ।

अथ कथम्—

अक्षं विक्षिपति ध्वजं दलयते मृद्नाति नद्धं युगं
चक्रं चूर्णयति क्षिणोति तुरगान् रक्षःपतेः पक्षिराट् ।
रुन्धन् गर्जति तर्जयत्यभिभवत्यालम्बते ताडय-
त्याकर्षत्यवलुम्पति प्रचलति न्यञ्चत्युदञ्चत्यपि ॥

(हनुमन्नाटके ४-११)

इत्यत्र तर्जयतीति प्रयोगः । तर्जतेश्चौरादिकस्य अनुदात्तेत्त्वादात्मनेपदेन भवितव्यम् । अत्राहुः[172]—चौरादिकस्य भौवादिकस्य वा हेतुमण्णिचि रूपमिदं भवतीति । एतेन

तर्जयन्निव केतुभिः (रघुवंशे ४-२८)

इति प्रयोगोऽपि [173]व्याख्यातः

अथ कथम्—

त्रपामपाकृत्य निभान्निभालय क्षितिक्षितं मालयमालयं रुचः

(नैषधे १२-५३)

इति श्रीहर्षस्य प्रयोगः । भल [174]आभण्डने इत्यस्य चौरादिकस्य (आकुस्मादात्मनेपदिनः इत्यनेन) आत्मनेपदित्वात् कथं परस्मैपदप्रयोगः—इति चेत्—अत्र [175]केचित् निभालनं निभालः । तद्वान् निभालवान् । तादृशं कुरु इति तत्करोतीति णिचि मतुपो लोपे च साधनीयमिति वदन्ति ।

171. Mallinātha on *Māgha* VI.4 gives the same answer.

172. See *P.M.* on the root *tarja* in *Curādi*.

173. See *K.A.S.*V.2.3, and the *Vṛtti* thereon. See also Mallinātha on *Raghu*.IV.28.

174. Bhaṭṭoji notes in his *P.M.*: *ābhaṇḍanam=nirūpaṇam*. Nirūpaṇa is in the sense of seeing or ascertaining.

175. This seems to be a reference to Nārāyaṇa. See his commentary on *Naiṣadha* XII.53, where the exact wording is found.

See also Mallinātha on *Naiṣadha* XI.1. He has a different way of justification too.

अथ कथम्—

स्रक् पारिजातस्य ऋते नलाशां वासैरशेषामपुपूरदाशाम्

(नैषधे ६-८६)

इति श्रीहर्षः ।

अत्र पूरी आप्यायने इति चौरादिकस्येदं रूपमिति वक्तव्यम् । तत्र णिचि कृते णौ चङ्युपधाया (७-४-१) इति ह्रस्वे च दीर्घो लघोः (७-४-९४) इत्यनेन अभ्यासस्य दीर्घेण भवितव्यम् । अपूपुरद् इति रूपेण च भाव्यम्—

अचूचुरच्चन्द्रमसोऽभिरामताम् (माघे १-१६)

इति यथा । इति चेत्—सत्यम् । प्रामादिकमेवेदमिति ऋजुदृशः । न च नाग्लोपि—(७-४-२) इत्यनेन दीर्घस्य निषेध इति वाच्यम् । अस्य धातोरग्लोपित्वाभावात् । केचित्तु संज्ञापूर्वको विधिरनित्य इति परिभाषया दीर्घो नेति कथंचित् [176]समाधेयमित्याहुः । अथ वा पूरी आप्यायने इत्यस्य घञि पूरणमित्यर्थे पूरः । ततस्तत् करोतीति (गणसूत्रेण) णिचि अग्लोपित्वात् नाग्लोपीति (७-४-२) इत्यनेन दीर्घनिषेधे इदं रूपमिति वा समाधेयमिति च ।

अथ कथम्—

मातर्जगज्जननि पद्मकृताधिवासे कोपं प्रशामय हरेर्मुरमर्दनस्य ।
नो चेत्त् चिरं रचितचारुचराचरस्य सक्रोधवीक्षणवशाद् भविता विनाशः ॥

इति [177]नरसिंहचम्पूकाव्ये । अत्र णिजन्तस्य शमिधातोरमन्तत्वेन जनीजृष्—(गणसूत्रम् १८८) इत्यनेन मित्संज्ञायाम् मितां ह्रस्वः (६४-९२) इति उपधायाः ह्रस्वः स्यात् । तेन च प्रशमयेति भाव्यम् ।

न च शमो दर्शने (गणसूत्रम्) इत्यनेन मित्वस्य प्रतिषेध इति वाच्यम् । तत्र शाम्यतिश्चक्षुर्जन्यदर्शने मिन्न स्यादित्यर्थनियमात्[178] । प्रकृते च चक्षुर्जन्यदर्शनाभावात् मित्संज्ञा वज्रलेपायते इति चेत्—अत्राहुः[179] । नायं शम उपशमे इत्यस्य प्रयोगः । किं तु शम आलोचने इति चौरादिकस्य । अमन्तत्वलक्षण-

176. See Nārāyaṇa's commentary on *Naiṣadha* VI.86.

177. I am unable to verify the work. Sūryakavi, the author of a commentary *Bālabodhikā* on the *Kavikalpalatā* of Deveśvara, is said to have written also a *Narasiṃhacampū*. See S.K. De's *H.S.P.*, p. 262. It is not clear whether the reference here is to this *Narasiṃhacampū*, which is possible. See the Introduction. See also Note 230-b.

178. See *S.K.* under *śamo'darśane*, a *gaṇasūtra* in *ghaṭādi* (in *Bhavādi*).

179. Bhaṭṭoji has these explanations. All the twisting and jugglery mean in simple terms that these usages have been regarded as correct, irrespective of the recordings in the remote past, which may appear contrary.

मित्संज्ञा तु चौरादिकस्य नास्ति । नान्ये मितोऽहेतौ (गणसूत्रम् १९७)) इत्यनेन ज्ञपादिपञ्चकव्यतिरिक्तानां चुरादीनाम् अहेतौ स्वार्थे णिचि मित्संज्ञानिषेधात् ।

नन्वेकं सन्धित्सतोऽपरं[179a] प्रच्यवते इतिन्यायेन निशामय प्रशामयेति रूपसिद्धावपि परस्मैपदित्वहानिः प्राप्नोति । शम आलोचने इत्यस्य आकुस्मादात्मनेपदिनः इति (गणसूत्रेण) आत्मनेपदविधानात् इति चेत्—सत्यम् । अत्र [180]वदन्ति-स्वार्थण्यन्तात् हेतुमण्णिचि रूपमिदमिति साधनात् । न चार्थासंगतिः । नित्तृप्रेषणाद् धातोः प्राकृतेर्थे णिजिष्यते इति सिद्धान्तात् । धातूनामनेकार्थत्वाच्च उपशमादौ वृत्तिरिति च । एतेन

निशामय तदुत्पत्तिं विस्तराद् गदतो मम (१-२)

इति देवीमाहात्म्यमपि व्याख्यातम् ।

अथ कथम्—

ततः [181]समाज्ञापयदाशु सर्वानानायिनस्तद्विचये नदीष्णान् (रघुवंशे १६-७५)

इति कालिदासः ।

अत्र मारणतोषण निशामनेषु ज्ञा (गणसूत्रम्) इत्यनेन निशामनार्थे जानाते-र्मित्त्वविधानात् मितां ह्रस्वः (६-४-९२) इत्यनेन ह्रस्वः स्यात् (तेन समाज्ञपयत्) इति भवितव्यम् इति चेत्—उच्यते । निशामनं चाक्षुषज्ञानमिति माधवः[182] । तन्मते अचाक्षुषज्ञाने मित्वाभावान्न दोषः । ज्ञापनमात्रे मित्वमिति मते तु नेदं जानातेः रूपम् । किं तु ज्ञा नियोगे इति चौरादिकस्य । धातूनामनेकार्थत्वाच्च नियोगव्यतरिक्तार्थेऽपि वृत्तिः । हरदत्तादयस्तु [183]निशानेष्विति पाठं स्वीकृत्य निशानं तीक्ष्णीकरणमिति व्याख्याय प्रकृते तदभावात् जानातेरेवेदं रूपमित्युक्तावपि न दोष इत्याहुः । वृत्तिकारस्तु मितां ह्रस्वः (६-४-९२) इत्यत्र वा चित्तविरागे (६-४-९१) इत्यतो वाग्रहणमनुवर्त्य [184]व्यवस्थितविभाषामङ्गीचकार । एतेन

अथ यन्तारमादिश्य धुर्यान् विश्रामयेति सः (रघु—१-५४)

इति

रजो विश्रामयन् राज्ञाम् (४-८५)

इत्यादि च व्याख्यातम् ।

179-a. This is also known as "*Ekam anusandhitsataḥ*" etc. See *laukikanyāyāñjali*; by G.A. Jacob; N.S.P., 1925.

180. See *P.M.* under *śama ālocane* in *Curādi*.

181. See *S.K.* under *Māraṇatoṣaṇa*-etc. in *Ghaṭādi*. Bhaṭṭoji also quotes: *vijñāpanā bhartṛṣu siddhim eti*; (*Kumāra*-VII.93)
and *Taj jñāpayaty ācāryaḥ* (*Mahābhāṣya*, many places)
These are quoted earlier by Haradatta on 1.4.34.

182. Bhaṭṭoji has a good discussion about this in his *S.K.* under *Māraṇatoṣaṇa*-etc.

183. See *Padamañjarī* on 1.4.34.

184. See *Kāśikā* 6.4.92. Also see *Durghaṭavṛtti* on the same.

अथ पदव्यवस्था[185]

अथ कथम्—

एतन्मन्दविपक्वतिन्दुकफलश्यामोदरापाण्डर-
प्रान्तं हन्त पुलिन्दसुन्दरकरस्पर्शक्षमं लक्ष्यते ।
तत् पल्लीपतिपुत्रि कुञ्जरकुलं कुम्भाभयाभ्यर्थना-
दीनं त्वामनुनाथते कुचयुगं पत्रावृतं माकृथाः ॥

(काव्यप्रकाशे ७मोल्लसे उद्धृतम्)

इत्युदाहरणे काव्यप्रकाशर्दाशते अनुनाथते इति प्रयोगः । आशिषि नाथः इति वार्त्तिकेन[186] आशीरर्थे एवात्मनेपदमिति नियमात् । अत्र च तदभावात् कथमयं प्रयोगः इति चेत्—सत्यम् । प्रमाद एवायम् । तेन अनुनाथति स्तनयुगम् इति पठनीयमिति काव्यप्रकाशकारः । न च आशिष्येवेति नियमे अन्यत्र नाथते-रात्मनेपदस्य प्रयोगाभावे अनुदात्तेत्त्वं तस्य व्यर्थमिति वाच्यम् । अनुदात्तेतश्च हलादेः (३-२-१४६) इतिविहितस्य युच्प्रत्ययस्य [187]प्रवृत्त्यर्थत्वात् । तेन नाथन इति रूपं सिद्ध्यति ।

अथ कथम्—

(धन्यासि या कथयसि प्रियसंगमेऽपि विस्रब्धचाटुकशतानि रतान्तरेषु ।)
नीवीं प्रति प्रणिहिते तु करे प्रियेण सख्यः शपामि यदि किंचिदपि स्मरामि ॥

(विज्जिकाया इति शार्ङ्गधरपद्धतिः)

इति काव्यप्रकाशोदाहृते शपामीति प्रयोगः ।

शप उपालम्भे इतिवार्त्तिकेन (अपाच्चतुष्पादित्यादिसूत्रव्याख्याने कौमुद्यां दृश्यताम्) अकर्तृगेऽपि फले शपथरूपार्थे आत्मनेपदस्य विहितत्वात् ।

185. *Pada* stands for *Ātmanepada* and *Parasmaipada*.

In the previous portion too there was a discussion about the correctness of a particular *pada*. For instance, in *anuktam apy ūhati paṇḍito janaḥ*, the correctness of *parasmaipada* was questioned because it was against the usual *ātmanepada* of the root *ūha vitarke*. The point to be noted in this context is this. The root *ūha* is always *ātmanepadin* as recorded and handed down by the tradition. In the following portion the author discusses about the use of one instead of the other, where both *padas* are allowed, but only in specific meanings.

186. See *Ś.K.* on 1.3.21. Bhaṭṭoji quotes here: *nāthase kimu patim na bhūbhṛtām* (*Kirāta*-XIII.59), and also gives this answer.

187. See *Ś.K.* on 1.3.21 and *T.B.* on the *Vārttika Āśiṣi nāthaḥ* (on the rule 1.3.21), where this point is also mentioned.

अयि शपे हृदयाय तवैव तद् यदि विधो र्न रुचेरसि गोचरः

(नैषधे ४-१०६)

इति श्रीहर्षप्रयोगवदात्मनेपदमेव युक्तम् । तत् कथमत्र परस्मैपदप्रयोगः इति चेत्—अत्र [188]वदन्ति—स्वाभिप्रायप्रकाशनमिह विवक्षितम् । न शपथरूपोऽर्थ इति ।

अथ कथम्—

व्यादत्ते विहगपतिर्मुखं स्वकीयम्

इति प्रयोगः । आङो दोऽनास्यविहरणे (१-३-२०) इत्यनेन मुखविकसनादन्यत्रैव आङ्पूर्वस्य ददातेरात्मनेपदविधानात् । प्रकृते च मुखप्रसारणार्थत्वात् । कथमत्रात्मनेपदम् इति चेत्—अत्र [189]वदन्ति धातोरुभयपदित्वं तु स्थितम् । अनेन सूत्रेण अकर्त्रभिप्रायेऽपि तद्विधानं क्रियते । कर्त्रभिप्रायत्वे तु स्वत एवात्मनेपदं स्वरितञितः (१-३-७२) इत्यनेन सिद्धम् । तदिह भविष्यतीति ।

अथ कथम्—

स्तुत्यं स्तुतिभिरर्थ्याभिरुपतस्थे सरस्वती (रघु-४-६) इति प्रयोगः । उपाद्देवपूजासंगतिकरणेत्यादिवार्त्तिकेन (१-३-२५ सूत्रं दृश्यताम्) उपात्परस्य तिष्ठतेर्देवपूजार्थे एव तङो विधानात् । अत्र स्तुत्यं नृपम् इति मनुष्ययोगे कथमिति चेत्—अत्र [190]वदन्ति नृपतेर्देवतात्वारोपात् । नृपस्य देवांशत्वाद् वा इति ।

अथ कथम्—

आजघ्ने विषमविलोचनस्य वक्षः (किरात–१७-६३)

इति भारविः । आङो यमहनः (१-३-२८) इतिसूत्रे अकर्मकात् स्वाङ्गकर्मकादित्येव इत्यर्थनियमात् । इह चार्थद्वयस्याप्यभावात् कथमात्मनेपदमिति चेत्—प्रमाद एवायमिति [191]भागवृत्तिः । रावणं प्राप्येत्यध्याहृत्य वा व्याख्येयमित्याहुः । न च प्राप्येत्यध्याहारे ल्यब्लोपे पञ्चमी स्यात् । प्रासादमारुह्य प्रेक्षते इत्यर्थे प्रासादात् प्रेक्षते इतिवत् इति वाच्यम् । ल्यबन्तं विनैव तदर्थावगति र्यत्र तद्विषयत्वात् [192]तत्पञ्चम्याः ।

अथ कथम्—

निर्गतं सुमहत् तेजस्तच्चैक्यं समगच्छत (देवीमाहात्म्ये–२-११)

188. *Ś.K.* has this answer (1.3.21).
189. See *Ś.K.* on 1.3.20.
190. See *Ś.K.* on 1.3.25.
191. *Ś.K.* on 1.3.28 has the discussion.
192. See *S.K.* on 1.3.28.

इति प्रयोगः। अत्र समो गम्यृच्छिभ्याम् (१-३-२९) इति सूत्रेण अकर्मकादेव-तङो विधानात्। प्रकृते च गमेः सकर्मकत्वात्—इति चेत् आर्षत्वादित्याहुः[193]। अथ वा ऐक्यमिति चार्तुर्वर्ण्यादित्वात् (७-३-३१ सूत्रे कौमुदी दृश्यताम्) स्वार्थे ष्यञ्ञि रूपम्। ऐक्यं एकं समगच्छत समपद्यत इति वा समाधेयमिति च।

अथ कथम्—

रक्षांसीति पुरापि संशृणुमहे वीरस्तु कस्तादृशो
जागर्ति स्म जगत्त्रयीविपदलंकर्मीणदोर्विक्रमः।

(अनर्घराघवे ६-२५)

इति मुरारिप्रयोगः। अर्तिश्रुदृशिभ्यश्चेति वक्तव्यम् (१-३-२९ सूत्रे दृश्यताम्) अकर्मकादित्येवेत्यर्थनियमात्। प्रकृते च शृणोतेः सकर्मकत्वात् कथमात्मनेपदम् इति चेत्—प्रमाद एवायमित्याहुः[194]। इति कथयदभ्य इत्यध्याहारो वे इति च।

अथ कथम्—

नभः समाक्रामति[195] चन्द्रमाः क्रमात्

इति प्रयोगः। अत्र आङ उद्गमने (१-३-४०) इतिसूत्रेण आङ्पूर्वस्य क्रमतेः उद्गमनार्थे आत्मनेपदविधानात् इति चेत्—सत्यम्। व्याप्तिमात्रमिह विवक्षितम्। न तूद्गमनम्। तेन न तङ [196]इत्याहुः।

अथ कथम्—

तव भ्रूकालिन्दीतनुतरतरङ्गायततले
कृतावासं मीनद्वयमिति वदे तेऽम्ब नयने-इति लावण्यलहरिः ?।

अत्र परस्मैपदिनो वदतेः कथमात्मनेपदप्रयोगः इति चेत्—एवं वदन्ति[197] भासनोपसंभाषा ज्ञानेत्यादिसूत्रेण (१-३-४७) भासनाद्यर्थविवक्षया समाधेयमिति।

अथ कथम्—

भुङ्क्ते श्रितश्रोत्रियसात्कृतश्रीः
पूर्वं त्वहो शेषमशेषमन्त्यम् (नैषधे ३-२५)

इति श्रीहर्षः। अत्र भुजपालनाभ्यवहारयोरिति धातोः भुजोऽनवने (१-३-६६)

193. See *Ś.K.* on 1.3.29.

194. *Ś.K.* has this (1.3.29).

195. See *Durghaṭavṛtti* on 1.3.40, which quotes the following:
nabhas samākrāmati naṣṭavartmanā
sthitvaikacakreṇa rathena bhāskaraḥ.

196. Bhaṭṭoji quotes the same line in his *Ś.K.* on 1.3.40.

197. See also *Naiṣadha* XIV.36, and the *Nalakīrtikaumudī* (my edition) II.31, & II.34.

इति सूत्रेण रक्षणव्यतिरिक्तार्थे ओदनं भुङ्क्ते इत्यादावेव आत्मनेपदविधानात् । इह तु तदभावात् परस्मैपदेन भवितव्यम् इति चेत्—सत्यम् । इहोपभोग एव भुजेरर्थः । न पालनमिति समादधुः ।

अथ कथम्—

इत्थं नृपः पूर्वमवालुलोचे ततोऽनुजज्ञे गमनं सुतस्य

(भट्टिकाव्ये १-२३)

इति प्रयोगः । अत्र स्वत उभयपदिनोऽपि जानातेः अनुपसर्गाज्ज्ञः (१-३-७६) इतिसूत्रेण जानातेर्यदि तङ तर्हि अनुपसर्गदिवेत्यर्थनियमात् । प्रकृते सोपसर्गात् कथमात्मनेपदप्रयोगः इति चेत्—सत्यम् । अनुजज्ञे इति नायं कर्तरि तङ । किं तु कर्मणि । ततः सोपसर्गादपि तत्संभवात् । तदा नृपेणेति विभक्तिविपरिणामः कार्य [198]इत्याहुः ।

अथ कथम्—

किंशुकमुखमनुकुरुते कामार्तिं वदति दुस्सहं धीरः ।
किंनरगीतं मधुरं किंपुरुषमुखं तुरङ्गमुखसदृशम् ॥ इति ॥

आज्ञा न त्रिपुरान्तकस्य गणिता देवः स्मरो निन्दितो
बन्धूनां वचनं विलङ्घितमतः पापस्य विच्छित्तये ।
देहो भूशयनव्रतं वितनुते पाथोनिवासव्रतं
चक्षुः स्वीकुरुते मनोऽनुकुरुते तापाग्निवासव्रतम् ॥

इति भानुकरमिश्रः[199] । अत्र अनुपूर्वात् करोतेः कर्तृगेऽपि क्रियाफले अनुपराभ्यां कृञः (१-३-७९) इति सूत्रेण परस्मैपदस्य विधानात् कथमत्रात्मनेपदम् इति चेत्— सत्यम् । प्रमाद एवायमिति बहवः । संज्ञापूर्वको विधिरनित्य इत्यनेन वा परस्मैपदाभावः समाधेयः इति वदन्ति ।

अथ कथम्—

निपीयतां नाम चकोरजिह्वया कथंचिदेतन्मुखचन्द्रचन्द्रिका ।
इमां किमाचामयसे न चक्षुषी चिरं चकोरस्य भवन्मुखस्पृशी ॥

(नैषधे १२-६)

198. See *Jayamaṅgalā* on Bhaṭṭi I.23, and also the *Ś.K.* on 1.3.76.

199. MSS. A, & E read: Bhānukaramandraḥ.

MS. F reads: Bhānukarabhūḥ.

MSS. B, C, D, & G read: Bhānukaramiśraḥ, who is said by some to be identical with Bhānudatta. For the controversy. See P.V. Kane's *H.S.P.* (p.360). I have not been able to trace the verses.

इति श्रीहर्षः । अत्र कर्त्रभिप्रायक्रियाफलविवक्षायाम् णिचश्च (१-३-७४) इतिसूत्रेण प्राप्तेऽप्यात्मनेपदे निगरणचलनार्थेभ्यश्च (१-३-८७) इत्यनेन भक्षणार्थानां परस्मैपदस्यैव नियमेन विधानमिति स्थितिः । अदेः प्रतिषेधः इति वार्त्तिकेन केवलमद भक्षणे इत्यस्यैव तत्प्रतिषेधः । तेन आङ्पूर्वस्य चमेः परस्मैपदमेव युक्तमिति चेत्—अत्र [200]वदन्ति । प्रमाद एवायमिति केचित् इति । अन्ये तु[201] आचामय इति लोडन्तं भङ्क्त्वा किं नाचामयेः इत्यर्थो व्याख्येय इति । अस्मिन् पक्षे से इति संबोधनम् । अस्य स्त्री ई । तया सह वर्तमाना से सयौ सयः । ततः हे से हे सलक्ष्मीके दमयन्तीत्यर्थः इति । पुनरपरे आचमनमाचामः । सोऽस्याः अस्तीति आचामवती । ततः तत्करोतीति णिचि मतुब्लोपे च आचामयसे इति कथंचित् साधनीयमिति[202] वदन्ति । न च निगरणचलनार्थेभ्यः इति निषेधः स्यादिति वाच्यम् । लक्षणप्रतिपदोक्तयोः प्रतिपदोक्तस्यैव ग्रहणमिति परिभाषया लाक्षणिके न प्रवृत्तिरत्रेति समाधेयम् ।

अथ कथम्—

हरेर्यदक्रामि पदैककेन खं पदैश्चतुर्भिः क्रमणेऽपि तस्य नः

(नैषधे १-७०)

इति श्रीहर्षः । अत्र क्रमतेः कर्मणि लुङि नोदात्तोपदेशस्य मान्तस्यानाचमेः (७-३-३४) इत्यनेन वृद्धिनिषेधात् अक्रमि इति भवितव्यम् । तत् कथम् अक्रामीति प्रयोगः इति चेत्—सत्यम् । प्रमाद एवायमिति बहवः[203] । निवृत्तप्रेषणाद् धातोः प्राकृतेऽर्थे णिजिष्यते इत्यनेन वा हेतुमण्णिचि वृद्धौ सत्यां क्रामीति रूपम् । ततः अक्रामीति [204]साधनीयम् इति ।

200. See Nārāyaṇa on *Naiṣadha* XII.6.
201. See *Ś.K.* on 1.3.87. Bhaṭṭoji notes this answer.
202. This is given by Nārāyaṇa on *Naiṣadha* XII.6.
203. See Nārāyaṇa on *Naiṣadha* I.70.
204. See *T.B.* on 7.3.34. The answer given here by having recourse to *nivṛttapreṣaṇād dhātoḥ* etc. was perhaps noted in the *P.M.* too. See however *P.M.* at the end of *Ṇijanta*, p. 475 (also p. 447).

अथ कृत्-प्रत्ययानुसारेण लिख्यते

अथ कथम्—

तं देशं विशति विभाण्डकस्य सूनौ
संदेशं बलमथनस्य संदधानः ।
पर्जन्यः प्रकटमगर्जदम्बरस्थो
वर्ष्टारं तमभिननन्द पौरबृन्दम् ॥
(उदारराघवे २-५)

इत्यत्र वर्ष्टारमिति प्रयोगः । वृषु सेचने इति धातोः (भौवादिकस्य) ण्वुल्-तृचौ (३-१-१३३) इति सूत्रेण तृचि कृते आर्धधातुकस्येड्वलादेः (७-२-३५) इत्यनेन इडागमे वर्षितारमिति स्यादिति चेत्—सत्यम् । प्रमाद एवायमित्येके । केचित्तु—निलोट्—इत्येव सिद्धे आनि लोट् (८-४-१६) इति सूत्रकरणात् ज्ञापकात् आगमशास्त्रमनित्यम्[205] । ततश्च प्राप्तोऽपि इडागमो न भवतीति समादधुः ।

अथ कथम्—

मयाङ्ग पृष्टः कुलनामनी भवानमू विमुच्यैव किमन्यदुक्तवान् ।
न मह्यमत्रोत्तरधारयस्य किं ह्रियेऽपि सेयं भवतोऽधमर्णता ॥
(नैषधे ६-३)

इति श्रीहर्ष प्रयोगः । अत्रोत्तरं धारयतीति विग्रहे अनुपसर्गाल्लिम्पविन्दधारीतिसूत्रं (३-१-१३८) विप्रतिषेधे परं कार्यम् (१-४-२) इतिपरिभाषासूत्रबलाद् बाधित्वा कर्मण्यण् (३-२-१) इतिसूत्रविहितः अण्प्रत्ययः प्राप्नोति । ततश्च सूत्रधारादिवद् रूपं स्यात् इति चेत्—सत्यम् । अत्राहुः । कर्मणः शेषत्वविवक्षायाम् अणः अप्राप्त्या अनुपसर्गेतिसूत्रविहिते शे(प्रत्यये) कृते शेषषष्ठ्यन्तेन समासो भविष्यतीति[206] ।

205. The *Nyāsakāra* notes this *Paribhāṣā* on 8.4.16, and quotes the usage: *api śākaṃ pacānasya sukhā vai maghavan gṛhāḥ*.

See also the *P.M.*, & *T.B.* on 8.4.16. *Durghaṭavṛtti* also notes this *Paribhāṣā* on 7.2.35. These writers give the example: *sāgaraṃ tartukāmasya* also.

Nāgeśa in his *Paribhāṣenduśekhara* rejects this *Paribhāṣā*. There is no reference to this rejection by our author. See also Note 57, and the Introduction.

206. *Ś.K.* on 3.1.138 has the discussion on this. Bhaṭṭoji also notes: *etena gaṅgādhara-bhūdhara-jaladharādayo vyākhyātāḥ*. See also *S.K.* on 3.2.1. See Mallinātha on Māgha IV.18. See also Note 216.

अथ कथम् —

जलगृहकवितर्दिकासुखानि स्फटिकगिरिर्गिरिशस्य निर्मिमीते

(अनर्घराघवे ७-४७)

इति मुरारिप्रयोगः । अत्र गिरौ शेते इति विग्रहे गिरौ डश्छन्दसि इति वार्त्तिकेन (३-२-१५ सूत्रस्थेन) विहितस्य डप्रत्ययस्य छन्दोविषयत्वात् । तत् कथं गिरिश इति प्रयोग इति चेत्—सत्यम् । [207]गिरिरस्यास्तीति विग्रहे लोमादि-पामादिपिच्छादिभ्यः शनेलचः (५-२-१००) इत्यनेन मत्वर्थे शप्रत्यये (लोमश इतिवत्) गिरिश इति रूपं व्याख्येयमिति [208]वदन्ति ।

अथ कथम्—

तस्य स्तनप्रणयिभिर्मुहुरेणशावैर्व्याहन्यमानहरिणीगमनं पुरस्तात् ।
आविर्बभूव कुशगर्भमुखं मृगाणां यूथं तदग्रसरगर्वितकृष्णसारम् ॥

(रघुवंशे ६-५५)

इति प्रयोगः । अत्र पुरोऽग्रतोऽग्रेषु सर्तेः (३-२-१८) इतिसूत्रेण टप्रत्यये अग्रेसर इति पदं सिद्धयति । तत्र हि अग्रम् अग्रेण अग्रे वा सरतीत्यर्थात् अग्रे इत्यव्यय-पूर्वपदत्वे स्वयमेदन्तत्वम् । अग्रशब्दपूर्वपदत्वे तु तस्य एदन्तत्वं निपात्यते इति कृत्वा अग्रेसर इति भाव्यम् । तत् कथमग्रसर इति प्रयोगः । कृत्यल्युटो बहुलम् (३-३-११३) इति बहुलग्रहणादेत्वाभाव इति [209]हरदत्तः समादधौ ।

अथ कथम्—

(गिरिस्तु कनकाचलः कति न सन्ति चाश्मव्रजाः
किटिस्तु धरणीधरः कति न सन्ति भूदारकाः ।
मरुत्तु मलयानिलः कति न सन्ति झञ्झानिलाः)
[210]प्रभुस्तु विबुधाश्रयः कति न सन्ति कुक्षिम्भराः ॥

207. See *P.M.* on 3.2.15. Bhaṭṭoji quotes several uses of *girīśa* and explains the point well. He also notes: *loke ayam (girīśaśabdaḥ) taddhitānta eva. na kṛdantaḥ. evaṃ ca girīśaśabdaṃ prayuñjānānāṃ kavīnāṃ na ko'py aparādhaḥ. girau śete iti vyācakṣāṇānāṃ tu pramāda ity avadheyam.*

Under 3.2.15 Kaiyaṭa quotes:

vairavāsiṣṭhagirīśāḥ etc. (*Vākyapadīya* II.173)

See Nageśa's *Uddyota* for the meaning of the *kārikā*.

208. *Durghaṭavṛtti* on 3.2.15 says:

chāndasā api kvacid bhāṣāyāṃ prayujyante iti rakṣitaḥ. (p. 65).

209. See *Padamañjarī*, *Ś.K.* & *S.K.* On 3.2.18.

210. This is the reading in MS G and in the *T.B.*

MS. A reads: *prabhur budhajanāśrayāḥ.*

MS. C reads: *tanur budha*-etc.

MS. F reads: *prabhur bahudhanāśrayaḥ.*

In others the portion is missing.

इति [211]ढक्कारामकविः। अत्र फलेग्रहिरात्मंभरिश्च (३-२-२६) इतिसूत्रे अनुक्तसमुच्चयार्थकचकारात् [212]कुक्षिंभरिरिति पदं सिद्धयतीति वृत्तावुक्तम् । अमरोऽप्याह—उभावात्मंभरिः कुक्षिंभरिः स्वोदरपूरके इति । प्रकृते कथं कुक्षिंभर इति प्रयोग इति चेत्—निरङ्कुशाः कवयः इति बहवः । [213]प्रामादिक एवायम् इत्येके । केचित्तु संज्ञायां भृतॄवृजिधारिसहितपिदमेः (३-२-४६) इतिसूत्रेण विहितस्य खच्-प्रत्ययस्य प्रवृत्तिम् (असंज्ञायामपि) आश्रित्य कथंचित्[214] समाधेयमित्याहुः[214a] ।

अथ कथम्—विष्णोर्जगत्क्षेमकरोऽवतारः (राघवपा ११-६)

इति कविराजः ।

अल्पारम्भाः क्षेमकराः इति च प्रयोगः ।

योगक्षेमकरं कृत्वा सीताया लक्ष्मणं ततः (भट्टिकाव्ये ५-५०)

इति भट्टिश्च । उभयत्रापि क्षेमप्रियमद्रे अण् च (३-२-४४) इतिसूत्रेण खचि प्रत्यये अणि वा प्रत्यये कृते क्षेमंकर इति क्षेमकार इति वा भाव्यम् । तत् कथं क्षेमकर इति चेत्—सत्यम् । उभयत्रापि क्षेमं करोतीति न विग्रहः । किं तु करोतीति कर इति पचाद्यचि (नन्दिग्रहीतिसूत्रेण ३-१-१३४) प्रथमं रूपम् । ततः कर्मणः शेषत्वविवक्षायां क्षेमस्य करः योगक्षेमयोः कर इति षष्ठीसमासः इत्याहुः[215] । एवमेव षष्ठीसमासमाश्रित्य [216]भूधरजलधरादयः प्रयोगा व्याख्येयाः ।

211. I am unable to get any information on this writer. See the Introduction. I have no means here of checking and finding out whether it could be a reference to Gururāmakavi of Diṇḍima family, the author of the *Ratneśvaraprasādana*, and other works. The date of Gururāma's *Hariścandra-carita-campū* is said to be 1607 A.D. See Introduction to *Ratneśavaraprasādana*; edn. by P.P.S. Sastri, Madras-1939.

212. In the *Mahābhāṣya* (3.2.26) we find:
kukṣyātmanor mum ca. Patañjali notes *kukṣiṃbhari*,
and quotes the line:
ātmaṃbhariś carati yūtham asevamānaḥ.
Kāśikā notes *udaraṃbhari*. See A.R. II.44.

213. This seems to be a reference to *T. B.*, from where perhaps our author quoted the usage also.

214. There is no other *śiṣṭaprayoga* so far known. This *kuksiṃbhara* was mistaken to be correct, probably on the analogy of Viśvaṃbhara. Viśvaṃbhara is a *saṃjñā* for Viṣṇu. But *kuksiṃbhara* is not noted as a *saṃjñā*.

214-a. Only MS. G has here a separate paragraph for *udaraṃbhari*, and quotes the usage: *jyotsnākarambham udaraṃbharayaś cakorāḥ* from Murāri (*A.R.* II.44). Others do not have the portion.

215. See *P.M.* and *S.K.* on 3.2.44, where *alpārambhāḥ kṣemakarāḥ* is quoted. Our author is explaining the second from Bhaṭṭi (V.50) also by the same method. *Jayamaṅgalā* and Mallinātha on Bhaṭṭi explain the usage by having recourse to the *paribhāṣā* : *grahaṇavatā prātipadikena tadanta-vidhir nāsti*. See the commentaries for the details.

216. See Note 206.

अथ कथम्—

पर्यङ्कतापन्नसरस्वदङ्कां लङ्कापुरीमप्यभिलाषि चित्तम् (नैषधे ३-६६)

इति श्रीहर्षः ।

मेरोर्मेदुरयन्ति संमदमधःसंपातिभिर्ज्योतिषाम्

(अनर्घराघवे ७-५४)

इति मुरारिश्च । अत्राभिलाषीत्यादौ सुप्यजातौ णिनिस्ताच्छील्ये (३-२-७८) इत्यनेन णिनिप्रत्यय इति वक्तव्यम् । तच्च न घटते । तथा हि अत्र वृत्तिकारः (३-२-७८) इत्थं व्याचष्टे—सुपीति वर्तमाने पुनः सुब्ग्रहणमुपसर्गनिवृत्त्यर्थम् । उत्प्रतिभ्यामाङि सर्तेरुपसंख्यानम् इति समनन्तरवार्त्तिकं व्याचक्षाणौ न्यासकारहरदत्तौ च इत्थमाहतुः—सुब्ग्रहणस्य चोपसर्गनिवृत्त्यर्थत्वादुपसर्गे न प्राप्नोतीति कृत्वा (सृधात्वर्थं) वचनमिदमारब्धमिति । अन्यधातुविषये तु सत्युपसर्गे णिनेरप्रयोगो ज्ञेयः इति । ततश्च अभिलाषि-संपातीत्यादौ कथं णिनेः प्रयोग इति चेत्—अत्र वदन्ति[217] । सोपसर्गादपि णिनिरिति निष्कर्षाद् वृत्तिकारादिमतमुपेक्ष्यमिति । तेन नात्र दोषः संभावनीयः ।

अथ कथम्—

ततस्तनयविप्लवं समवलोक्य लोकेश्वरः

प्रकोपदहनार्चिषा दश दिशः समुज्ज्वालयन्

इति भृगुवंशे[218] । समुज्ज्वालयन्नित्यत्र णिजन्ताज्ज्वल दीप्ताविति धातोः शतृप्रत्ययो वक्तव्यः । तत्र ज्वल-ह्वल-ह्मल-नमोऽनुपसर्गाद् वा (१८९) इति घटाद्यन्तर्गतगणसूत्रेण उपसर्गविशिष्टस्य नित्यं मित्संज्ञाविधानात् मितां ह्रस्वः (६-४-९२) इत्यनेन उपधायाः ह्रस्वप्राप्तया समुज्ज्वलयन्नित्येव रूपं स्यादिति चेत्—अत्राहुः[219] । ज्वलनं ज्वालः घञन्ते रूपम् । ततो घञन्तात् तत् करोति तदाचष्टे इति (चुराद्यन्तर्गतेन-२०४) गणसूत्रेण णिचि कृते ततः शतरि समुज्ज्वालयन्निति रूपं साधनीयमिति ।

अथ कथम्—

इत्युक्त्वा मैथिलीं भर्तुरङ्के निविशतीं भयात् ।

रूपं शूर्पणखा नाम्नः सदृशं प्रत्यपद्यत ॥ (रघुवंशे १२-३८)

217. This is a reference to Bhaṭṭoji. He has a good discussion in his *S.K.* on 3.2.78. He points out thus:

sarvathāpi sub-mātre upapade ṇiniḥ; na tv anupasarge eveti siddhāntah.

This is followed by *T.B.* also.

218. Except E, all the MSS. read clearly *Bhṛguvaṃśe*. I am unable to get any information about the author or the work.

219. Bhaṭṭoji raises this question in his *S.K.* (in *Ghaṭādi*) and answers thus: *katham tarhi prajvālayati unnāmayatīti. ghañantāt tat karotīti ṇau.*

इति कालिदासः । अत्र नेर्विशः (१-३-१७) इति सूत्रेण निपूर्वस्य विशते-रात्मनेपदविधानात् शानचा भाव्यम् (निविशमानाम् इति) इति चेत्—अत्राहुः । प्रमाद एवायमिति बहवः । अङ्गानि [220]विशतीं भयात् इति वा प्रामाणिकपाठ इति ।

अथ कथम्—

निघ्नानं शात्रवान् रामं कथं त्वं नावगच्छसि (भट्टिकाव्ये ५-८१)

इति भट्टिः । हन्तेः परस्मैपदित्वात् कथमत्र शानच् इति चेत्—नायं शानच् प्रत्ययः । किं तु ताच्छील्यवयोवचनशक्तिषु चानश् (३-२-१२९) इतिसूत्रेण ताच्छील्याद्यर्थे विहितः [221]शक्त्यर्थकोऽत्र चानश् । अयं हि परस्मैपदिनोऽपि संभवति । एतेन

शिवाग्नौ [222]जुह्वाना सुरभिघृतधाराहुतिशतैः (प-३३) इति सौन्दर्य-लहरीप्रयोगः (जुह्वाना इति) व्याख्यातः ।

अथ कथम्—

कथं न गन्ता विफलीभविष्णुतां
स्वयंवरः साध्वि समृद्धिमानपि ।। (नैषधे ९-८१)

इति श्रीहर्षः । भूष्णुर्भविष्णुर्भविता इत्यमरश्च । भुवश्च (३-२-१३८) इतिसूत्रेण विहितस्य इष्णुच्-प्रत्ययस्य छन्दोविषयत्वात् कथमत्र लोके प्रयोगः इति चेत्—प्रमाद एवेदृशप्रयोग [223]इत्याहुः ।

अथ कथम्—

वाचमूचे सुधाधारां मधुरां मधुसूदनः (चम्पूरामायणे बालकाण्डे २२ प-) इति । अत्र हि अनुदात्तेतश्च हलादेः (३-२-१४९) इति विहितस्य युच्-प्रत्ययस्य सूददीपदीक्षश्च (३-२-१५३) इत्यनेन सूदधातोः प्रतिषेधात् कथं मधुसूदन इति प्रयोग इति चेत्—सत्यम् । नायं युच् । किं तु नन्दिग्रहीत्यादिसूत्रेण (३-१-१३४) विहितः ल्युप्रत्ययः [224]इत्याहुः ।

220. See *P.M.* & *T.B.* on 1.3.17.
221. See *Jayamaṅgalā* and Mallinātha on Bhaṭṭi on V.81.
222. Some printed editions have *juhvantaḥ*. The commentaries too on the *Saundaryalaharī* read *juhvantaḥ*. See *Lakṣmīdharā* and *Aruṇāmodinī* (pp. 160 & 161; Gaṇesh and Co., Madras, 1957). The commentary *Saubhāgyavardhanī* mentiones about the reading *juhvānāḥ* as suggested by some. Bhaṭṭoji justifies it as correct. It is not clear who are meant by this. See *P. M.* & *T.B.* under the root *Hu*.
223. See *Padamañjarī* and *P.M.* on 3.2.138.
224. See S.K. on 3.2.153, and on 3.1.134.

अथ कथम्—

पीयूषाश्रपणं जगत्त्रयदृशामालातलेखालवो

विश्वोन्माथहुताशनस्य ककुभामुद्घाटनी कुञ्चिका। (अनर्घराघवे७-८३)

इति मुरारिः । अत्र ण्यासश्रन्थो युच् (३-३-१०७) इति सूत्रेण युच्-प्रत्यये उद्घाटनीति रूपमिति वक्तव्यम् । तत्र घटधातो र्घटादयो । मितः इत्यनेन मित्त्वात् मितां ह्रस्वः (६-४-९२) इत्यनेन ह्रस्वे उद्घटनीति स्यात्—इति चेत्— सत्यम् । नेदं घट चेष्टायाम् इत्यस्य रूपम् । किं तु घट संघाते इति चौरादिकस्य । तस्यैव मित्त्वार्थं घटादावनुवाद इति तु न भ्रमितव्यम् । तत्र नान्ये मितोऽहेतो (चुरादौ गणसूत्रम्-१९८) इत्यनेन निषेधात् । एतेन

"प्रविघाटयिता समुत्पतन् हरिदश्वः कमलाकरानिव" (किरातार्जुनीये २-४६)

इति भारविः

कमलवनोद्घाटनं कुर्वते ये (सूर्यशतके २)

इति मयूरः

उद्घाटनं घटीयन्त्रं सलिलोद्वाहनं प्रहेः

इत्यमरश्च व्याख्याताः ।

अथ कथम्—

चापे तातजटायुजीवितकथापर्यन्तधूमायित-

क्रोधोत्पीडनिपीतशोकजडिमा दृष्टिस्तु विश्राम्यति ॥

(अनर्घराघवे ५-१२)

इति मुरारिप्रयोगः ।

मा वधिष्ठा जटायुं माम् (भट्टिकाव्य ६-४१)

इति भट्टिप्रयोगः ।

तातो मद्विरहाग्निदग्धहृदयः प्राणान् परित्यक्तवान्

कान्तारेऽपि जटायुनापि मरणं प्राप्तं मदर्थे तथा ।

इति [225]रामविजये च ।

वायुना जगदायुना

इति [226]वर्णविवेकश्च । अत्र जटा आयुरस्येति विग्रहे छन्दसीणः (उणादि-सूत्रम्-२) इति विहितस्य उण्-प्रत्ययस्य छन्दोविषयत्वात् एतेर्णिच्च (उणादि-सूत्रम्-२७५) इतिविहितः उसि-प्रत्यय एव युक्तः । ततश्च

225. I am unable to get any information about the work Rāmavijaya or the author.

226. This Varṇaviveka is mentioned in the *T.B.* too (uṇādi-2-&-94). It is not clear which work is meant by this.

गृध्रं हत्वा जटायुषम् (रामायणे) इतिवत् सकारान्तेन प्रातिपदिकेन भवितव्यम् । न तु उकारान्तेन । तर्हि कथमेते प्रयोगा युज्यन्ते । एवं सन्देहे समाधानमिदं वदन्ति । छन्दसीण इति सूत्रविहितम् उण्-प्रत्ययं बाहुलकाद् भाषायामप्याश्रित्य उकारान्त आयुशब्दः साधनीय इति केचिदाहुः । दर्शितो भट्टिप्रयोगः

तटी-मध्येः पद्भ्याम-भजत जटायोः प्रथमजः (रामचरिते ६-४१) इत्यभिनन्दप्रयोगश्च अस्मिन्नर्थे प्रमाणमिति स्वीकुर्वन्ति । अन्ये तु जटां याति प्राप्नोति इति विगृह्य मृगय्वादयश्च (उणादिसूत्रम्-३७) इत्यनेन कु-प्रत्यये मृगयु-वत् आयुपदम् उकारान्तं साधनीय[227]मित्याहुः । एतेन आयुर्जीवितकालो ना इत्यमरः (उकारान्त आयुशब्द इत्यङ्गीकारेऽपि) जटायुषा जटायुश्च विद्यादायुं तथायुषा इति द्विरूपकोशश्च व्याख्यातो भवति ।

अथ कथम्—

विरुते कलकण्ठस्य मरुते वाति शीतले ।
त्वरते मानसं यूनां सुरते सुखसागरे ॥

इति कस्यचित् प्रयोगः ।

कोयं वाति स दाक्षिणात्यमरुतः इति [27a]कवि[2]राजस्य च । अत्र मृग्रोरुतिः (उणादिसूत्रम्-९४) इत्यनेन उति-प्रत्यये तान्तशब्दस्यैव सिद्धिः । नत्वदन्तस्य । तत् कथमीदृशप्रयोग इति चेत्—अत्राहुः । प्रमाद एवायमिति केचित् । दाक्षिणात्यपवन इति पाठः कल्पनीय इति च । अन्ये तु अदन्तोऽप्यव्युत्पन्नोऽस्ति मरुतशब्दः । तथा च विक्रमादित्यकोशे

मरुतः स्पर्शनः प्राणः समीरो मारुतो मरुत् इति ।

[228]संसारावर्तश्च । अत एव

हेमन्तदिवस इव समरुतः कोकिलः

इति केषांचित् श्लेषश्च संगच्छते । अत्र कोकिलपक्षे समो रुतः शब्दो यस्येति पक्षान्तरे च मरुतेन[229] सहित इति व्याख्या ।

अथ कथम्—

प्रतिपदमिति वारं वारमाघ्राय गन्धं
मधुमथनमहेला सा सखीरन्वपृच्छत ॥

(पारिजातहरणचम्प्वाम्-२-३५)

227. See *T.B.* under the *Uṇādisūtra* 2. Perhaps the *P.M.* too had the discussion. Monier Williams also notes the two forms of *āyu* and *āyus*.

227-a. I do not find it in the *Rāghavapāṇḍavīya*.

228. All the MSS read clearly *Saṃsārāvarta*. It was probably a lexicon. It is not clear to me.

229. Monier Williams also notes *maruta* (a-stem) in the sense of *marut*.

इति पारिजातहरणे।[230]

क्षोणीभर्त्रे वितर मुषितामात्मपालो महेलाम्[230a]—

इति च राघवपाण्डवीये (७-४१)।

प्रसभमिवाङ्गदविह्वला महेला इति कविराजस्य प्रयोगश्च।

गज इव परमहेलाविलासी इति [230b]कविकल्पलतायाम् (६२ पुटे)। अत्र सलिकल्यनिमहि-इत्यादिसूत्रेण (उणादि-५४) इलच्-प्रत्ययान्तस्यैव साधितत्वात्। कथं महेलेति चेत्—अत्राहुः महेलापि पृषोदरादित्वात् साधुरिति[231]। इदमपि वयं मन्यामहे—महस्य उत्सवस्य इला भूमिः मुख्यस्थानम्। यतः सर्वे भोगा वनिताधीना इति। महिलायां महेला च इति द्विरूपकोशश्च।

अथ कथम्—

जन्मेन किं सकलभोगनिदानभूतां
सन्मेनकासहचरीमपहाय बालाम्।
यन्मे हरं हरिणलाञ्छनचन्द्रचूडं
यन्मेदुरं त्रिपुरसूदनमन्तरेण॥

इति कविकल्पलतायाम् अक्बरीयकालिदासः[231a]। सर्वत्र नान्तस्यैव जन्म-

230. MSS. A, C & F read: *Pārijātaharaṇe*. MSS. B, & G read: *Pārijātāpaharaṇe*. In MSS. D & E the portion is missing. This is a reference to the *Pārijātaharaṇacampū* of Śeṣakṛṣṇa, who was Teacher of Bhaṭṭoji. Śeṣakṛṣṇa wrote also a commentary on the *Prakriyākaumudī* of Rāmacandra. The commentary is known as *Prakriyāprakāśa*. Bhaṭṭoji in his *Śabdakaustubha* on 1.1.8 (p. 114; C.S.S.) refers to it thus: *tad etat sakalam abhisandhāya prakriyāprakāśe gurucaraṇair uktam* etc.

230-a. In the *Rāghavapāṇḍavīya*, the word *mahelā* has two meanings. One is *mahatī ilā* , and the other is *vanitā*.

230-b. I had access to the *Kavikalpalatā* of Deveśvara, published by Asiatic Sociey of Bengal, Calcutta. This was not available in full. First part had the auto-commentary. In the second part, the colophon at the end of the 4th & 5th section in the third chapter reads the commentary as:

sūryakavirājakṛtā bālabodhikā.

This Sūryakavi is said to have written the *Narasiṃhacampū*. See Note 177 also. The auto-commentary explains *paramahelā-vilāsī* thus: *pareṣāṃ mahelā=strī*; *tasyā vilāsī*; and *paramā yā helā=līlā, tayā vilāsī.*

Upamitibhavaprapañcā of Siddharṣi also uses *mahelā* (p. 190).

231. See *S.K.* & *T.B.* on *Uṇādisūtra* 54. The T.B. quotes here:

paramahelārato'py apāradārikaḥ

and attributes the line to one *Damayantīkāvya*. *Bālamanoramā* attributes the same line to Śrīharṣa (?). I am unable to verify.

231-a. Except E, all MSS. read thus. Some verses attributed to Akbariyakālidāsa are noted by Haradatta Sharma, in the I.H.Q., Vol. X. (p. 484). This is not found there. I did not have access to the last part of the *Kavikalpalatā*. I do not know whether this verse is there. The connection of *Kavikalpalatā* and Akbarīyakālidāsa is also puzzling to me. I do not know whether the author of the former was also known by that name or title.

शब्दस्य दर्शनात् । कथमत्र अदन्तता इति चेत्—सत्यम् । अत एव किं जन्मनेति पठनीयमिति केचित् । अन्ये तु इषियुधीत्यादिसूत्रेण (उणादि-१४२) विहितस्य मक्-प्रत्ययस्य जन जनने इति धातोः आश्रयणात् जन्मम् इत्यप्यकारान्तं [232]भवतीत्याहुः । जनुर्जननजन्मानि इत्यमरोऽपि नकारान्ताकरान्तोभयसाधारणः । न चात्र नान्तत्वमेवास्त्विति वाच्यम् । साहचर्याच्च कुत्रचित् (अमरस्य) इति परिभाषया रूपसाहचर्यात् अदन्तसाहचर्यस्यापि क्वचिद् विवक्षितत्वात् । अर्चिर्हेतिः शिखा स्त्रियाम् इत्यत्र हेतिशब्दसाहचर्याद् अर्चिषः इकारान्तत्वमपि यथाङ्गीक्रियते तद्वत् । तस्मात् जननसाहचर्यात् जन्मशब्दस्य अदन्तत्वमपीति रायमकुटादयः । यन्मेदुरम् इत्यत्र यच्छब्दस्य यद्वेत्यर्थः ।

अथ कथम्—

कृतः पुरस्कृत्य ततो नलेन स प्रदक्षिणस्तत्क्षणमाशुशुक्षणिः ।

(नैषधे १६-३५)

इति श्रीहर्षप्रयोगः । अत्र आङि शुषेः सनश्छन्दसि (उणादि-२६०) इति साधितस्य छन्दोविषयत्वात् कथमत्र लोके प्रयोग इति चेत्—उणादयो बहुलम् (३-३-१) बहुलग्रहणाद् भाषायामपि प्रयुज्यते इति ।

अथ कथम्—

छर्द्यतीसारशूलवान् इति वैद्यशास्त्रम् । अर्चिशुचीत्यादिसूत्रेण (उणादि-२६५) विहितस्य इसि-प्रत्ययस्य सत्त्वात् प्रातिपदिकस्य (छर्दिस् इति) सान्तत्वस्यैव युक्तत्वात् इति चेत्—अत्राहुः । नायमिसिप्रत्ययान्ताः । किं तु अच इः (उणादि-५७८) इतिसूत्रेण इप्रत्यये (रविरितिवत्) इदन्तोऽप्ययमिति न दोष[233] इति ।

अथ कथम्—

गोपीकुचामर्दनकुङ्कुमाङ्कं गोरक्षकं गोरजधूसराङ्गम्—इति, प्रयोगः ।
प्रचकितस्मितमुग्धमुखस्तदा निजगुरुं समवेक्षत राघवः ।
अहह मामपि वेत्सि वरानने व्रतपरं तपरञ्जितकौशिकम् ॥

इति च रघूत्तमे [234]भ्रातृचरणाः । तथा

सहस्य प्रथमे मासि वाहयेद् दोषसंचयम् इति च ।

232. See *T.B.* on *Uṇādi*-142. This point is mentioned there. Probably it was in the *P.M.* too.

233. This is noted as such by Bhaṭṭoji. See *S.K.* on *Uṇādi*-265.

234. *Raghūttama* seems to be the name of a *kāvya*. It is a pity that the name of the brother, the author of this, is not mentioned.

अत्र रजशशब्दादीनां सान्तत्वेन प्रयोगदर्शनात् कथमदन्ततेति चेद्—अत्राहुः[235]। सर्वधातुभ्या-ऽसुन् (उणादि-६२८) इतिसूत्रेण रञ्ज रागे तप संतापे षह मर्षणे इत्येतेभ्यः असुन्प्रत्यये सान्तत्वमेषाम्। पचाद्यचि (नन्दिग्रहीतिसूत्रेण ३-१-१३४) घञर्थे कविधानमिति वार्त्तिकेन (ग्रहवृदृनिश्चीति सूत्रस्थेन (३-३-५८) कप्रत्यये अदन्तत्वमपि। भ्रातृचरणपद्ये तु तपरञ्जितकौशिकमित्यत्र तपशशब्दस्यादन्तत्वानुपपत्तिं मत्वा तपेन ग्रीष्मर्तुना रञ्जितकौशिकमिति रीत्या कैश्चित् कृतं क्लिष्टव्याख्यानं नादरणीयम्। व्रतरूपो यः परंतपः तेन रञ्जितकौशिकमिति व्याख्यानान्तरमपि न युक्तम्। द्विषत्परयोस्तापेः (३-२-३९) इत्यनेन धर्मिण्यर्थे एव खच्-प्रत्ययस्य विधानात्। वयं तु मन्यामहे—व्रतो ब्रह्मचर्यनियमः। तद्विषये तेन वा परम्—उत्कृष्टम्। तपेन—ब्रह्मध्यानादिना रञ्जितकौशिकम् इति। यद्वा-तप ऐश्वर्ये इति धातोः पूर्ववदचि तपेन—ऐश्वर्येण रञ्जितकौशिकमिति वा। भुवनाधिपतिरप्यहं त्वया सह गच्छामीत्येतादृशं तोषं विना किं तव तोषान्तरेणेति भावः। एतेषां शब्दानामदन्तत्वे द्विरूपकोशोऽपि संवादकः—यथा

नभं तु नभसा सार्धं तपं तु तपसा सह।
सहं तु [236]सहसा सार्धं रजेनापि समं रजः॥ इति।

अथ कथम्—

पिण्डं दद्याद् गयाशिरे इति वायव्यपुराणे प्रयोगः।
कुण्डलोद्घृष्टगण्डानां कुमाराणां तरस्विनाम्।
निचकर्त शिरान् द्रौणि र्नलिभ्य इव पङ्कजान्॥ इति महाभारते च।

अत्र असुन्-प्रकरणे श्रयतेः स्वाङ्गे शिरः किच्च (उणादि-६३६) इति सूत्रेण सान्तशब्दस्यैव व्युत्पादनात्। कथं प्रकृते अदन्तत्वमेतस्य इति चेत्—अत्र केचित् छन्दोवत् पुराणानि भवन्ति इत्याश्रित्य साधुत्वमदन्तत्वेऽपीत्याहुः। वस्तुतस्तु तस्मिन्नेव सूत्रे शॄहिंसायामिति धातोर्घञर्थे कप्रत्यये (घञर्थे कविधानमिति वार्त्तिकेन) ॠत इद्धातोः (७-१-१००) इत्यनेन इकारे अदन्तोऽपि शिरशब्दः इति [237]भाष्यज्ञाः। अत एव विक्रमादित्यकोशेऽपि

शिरोवाची शिरोऽदन्तो रजोवाची रजस्तथा—इति।

235. See *T.B.* on *Uṇādi*-628. It has the discussion on these words. It does not have illustrations for *adanta*-forms. Our author supplies the quotations for the uses.

236. *nabhas* (m) is *śrāvaṇamāsa*; and also the sky (neuter); *tapas* is austerity; *sahas* is *mārgaśirṣamāsa*; *rajas* is dust.

In all these meanings the words are thus shown to be possible with *a*-stems also.

237. See *T.B.* on *Uṇādi*-636. It has the discussion. Probably it was in the *P.M.* too.

अथ कथम्—

सर्वमापोमयं जगत्—इति प्रयोगः । आपोभिर्मार्जनं कृत्वा इति स्मृतिश्च । अप्-शब्दस्य पान्तत्वेन बहुत्वेनैव च प्रयोगदर्शनात् कथं सान्तप्रयोगः —इति चेत्— अत्राहुः । आपः कर्माख्यायाम् (उणादि-६४७) इतिसूत्रे बाहुलकात् सान्तत्वमन्य-वचनान्तत्वं चेति[238] । तथा च हलायुधः——

आपस्तोयं घनरसपयः पुष्करं मेघपुष्पम्
कं पानीयं सलिलमुदकं वारि वा शंबरं च ।
अर्णः पाथः कुशजलवनं क्षीरमम्भोऽम्बु नीरं
प्रोक्तं प्राज्ञैर्भुवनममृतं जीवनीयं दकं च ॥ (अभिधानरत्नमाला ३-२६)

अत्र आपशब्दस्य एकवचनसाहचर्यात् आप इत्येकवचनान्तमपि कोशकार-संमतम् । आपः स्त्री भूम्नि वार्वारी इत्यमरस्तु बहुप्रयोगाभिप्रायपर इति द्रष्टव्यम् ।

अथ कथम्—

विन्यस्तमङ्गलमहौषधिरीश्वरायाः
स्रस्तोरगप्रतिसरेण करेण पाणिः ॥ (किरातार्जुनीये ५-३३)

इति भारविः । अत्र अश्नोतेराशुकर्मणि वरट् च (उणादि-७३५) इति सूत्रेण वरट्-प्रत्यये उपधायाः ईत्वे च ईश्वर इति रूपम् । तस्य स्त्रियाम् टिड्ढाणञ् (४-१-१५) इत्यादिसूत्रेण टित्त्वात् ङीपि ईश्वरीति रूपं स्यात्—इति चेत्— सत्यम् । नायं वरट्-प्रत्ययान्तः येनोक्तदोषः स्यात् । किं तु स्थेशभासेत्यादिसूत्रेण (३-२-१७५) वरच्-प्रत्यये तस्य टित्त्वाभावात् न ङीप् । किं तु टाप् भवतीति न दोषः ।

इति सर्वं समञ्जसम् ।

(अन्ते एकस्मिन् [239]तालपत्रपार्श्वे स्थिताः काश्चन पंक्तयः अत्यन्तमस्फुटाः

238. See *S.K.* & *T.B.* on *Uṇādi*-647. These have the discussion.

239. The MS C has the discussion on the topics in this order:

(1) *subanta* (*-prakriyā*)

(2) *kṛdanta* (*-prakriyā*)

(3) *tiṅanta* (*-prakriyā*), this has a section as *padavyavasthā* (N.185) The portion dealing with *kṛt - pratyayas* is covered in MS. C from folio 19-a (end) to folio 26-b (beginning). The discussion on *tiṅ-pratyayas* begins on folio 27-a. Before this on folio 26-b of the MS. C alone there seem to have been lines which could not be copied, and this fact seems to be indicated by the scribe, who gives dot-like marks to show the gap. Other MSS. do not have these lines. These were only a few even in the MS. C, as is clear. As

लेखनप्रयत्नं न सफलयन्तीति लेखकस्य सूचनादवगम्यते ।)

([240]अत्र पंक्तीरिमाः केवलं वर्जयित्वा अवशिष्टग्रन्थः संपूर्ण इति च ज्ञायते ।)

इति शम् ।

a consequence, we can surmise that, excepting these few lines, the work is complete. Though other MSS do not have the colophon, the MS. A has at the end:

iti sāhityakaṇṭakoddhāraḥ samāptaḥ.

MS. F has...*uddhāram samāptam* (?). *asmin pustake kartṛnāma nāsti. tasmād atra na likhyate.*

See Note 149 for the different order of topics in other MSS.

240. This line is given by the Editor.

I. INDEX OF VERSES CITED

(in the *Sāhityakaṇṭakoddhāra*)

Final numbers refer to pages

II. INDEX OF EXPRESSIONS DISCUSSED

ADDITIONS AND CORRECTIONS

Page	*Line*	*Read*
XIX	9 (for item 2)	(P.58)
XX	32 (for item 29)	P.56
XXI	23	Delete p.50
8	3 of fn. 35	(*Ś.K.*, vol. I. .p127)
17	23	*grāmaṇīḥ*
18	8	*nalāśām*..,
22	25	*vārttikena* (dental "*na*")
26	1	" " "
29	20	" " "
28	18	*samāsā* - - (for *sāmā* - -)
29	11	*ata iñ*
35	25	*yathā = yogyatām*
47	7	*nivṛttapreṣaṇād*
50	11	*vā* (for "*ve*")
57	11	*juhvānāḥ*
58	5	*ghaṭādayo mitaḥ*
59	1	(*Rāmāyaṇe ?*)
59	6	Delete hyphens
59	16	Footnote number "227-a"
59	28	*anvapṛcchat*
62	24	*vārttikena*
64	1	Delete closing bracket
64	2	Delete beginning bracket
64	fn, 240	These lines are given by the Editor.
68	10	*patinā*